PRISON COOKBOOK 2

225 More Secrets from "The Inside"
Plus 25 Secrets from "The Outside"

Troy Traylor

Freebird Publishers

North Dighton, MA

Freebird Publishers
221 Pearl St., Ste. 541, North Dighton, MA 02764
Info@FreebirdPublishers.com
www.FreebirdPublishers.com

Copyright © 2020
Fine Dining Prison Cookbook 2
By Troy Traylor

All rights reserved. No part of this book may be reproduced in any form or by any means without the prior written consent of the Publisher, except in brief quotes used in reviews.

All Freebird Publishers titles, imprints, and distributed lines are available at special quantity discounts for bulk purchases for sales promotions, premiums, fundraising, educational, or institutional use.

ISBN: 978-1-952159-17-6

Printed in the United States of America

This book is dedicated to all my amazing friends and supporters, as well as to anyone who has a dream and will allow nothing to stop them from fulfilling it. To my son, Troy Neal Traylor, Jr. (TJ) and my daughter, Madeline Emma Traylor (Maddie): Even though we are miles apart, always remember – just because I'm not near you does not mean I'm not with you.

I love you more than you may ever know.

Acknowledgments

I sincerely want to thank everyone who has been part of my support team and helped make this dream, and many others, come true.

Kelsey Eiland and the Solitary Watch Organization: Kelsey, you are one of the most incredible human beings I have ever had the pleasure of meeting. Your love of life and love for others go beyond measure. You inspire me, encourage me, and love me more than I could ever deserve. Thank you for always seeing the good, no matter what the situation is. This world is a better place because you are in it.

Sister Jennifer and family: I truly thank you for adopting me and showing me how awesome life is. Your every word lifts me up and lets me know I am someone special. You have taught me to love and accept love in an unconditional way. You are an amazing family, and I am proud to share in this journey with you. One person at a time, you can, and will, change the world.

Sister Kay: I thank you for your dedication and ministry. You invited me to be part of a forever family, and I am so grateful for all you have done and continue to do.

Ms. Betty and all group members at Soul Sisters: Thank each of you for the parts you play in reminding me I am never forgotten. Each correspondence is full of laughs and materials that help you see how beautiful our world is. I hope each of you receives the same joy and love you freely give.

Brother James and Brother Ron: I am uplifted by your correspondence. I always know each letter is full of positive messages and a love that so many people fail to find in life. You have answered a calling that some don't hear. I love you guys and am proud to be your friend and Brother.

Natalie DeMarcus: What an amazing woman you are. You are genuine, pure, and true. I do not deserve a friend as loving as you. I am proud to be your friend and proud to call you my friend. You bring me much-needed joy, and my hope is that one day I get to hold you and show you my sincerity.

TJ: I want to thank you for your forgiveness and dedication to mending our relationship. It takes a man to do that, and I am proud you are my son.

Madeline: I want to encourage you to continue following your dreams and setting positive goals for yourself. Nothing can stop you if you allow nothing to stop you. I hope that the day comes when you can be as proud of me as I am of you.

Diane at Freebird Publishers: Thank you for taking on this project and working with me. I know I can be difficult, so your patience and expertise mean a lot to me. You and all your staff have done an amazing job.

Danny and Bonnie Cantrell: Thank you both for the years of love and emotional support. There is no possible way for me to show my gratitude. Just know that even though it may not always be seen, I love you both dearly.

Each of you has inspired me and supported me in many ways. Without your love and support, my dreams and this book would not be possible. I could never repay you for all you have done.

Last, but not least, let me say thank you to all the countless inmates who have shared experience, time, and recipes with me. Your help does not go unnoticed. I could never forget you. May the fulfillment of my dreams help you to fulfill your dreams.

Words to chew on: No matter who you are, where you are, or what you are, dreams do come true. *Never* let anyone or anything discourage you. Any failures you encounter today will be looked back on as experience later.

Preface

I have been on both sides of the fence. I have often been asked what it was like and what we ate. I have loved to cook and bake since I was a child, and have received many compliments, so I decided many years ago to put it on paper and share with everyone. You will simply be amazed at what a few simple ingredients will produce. Once you have read my books, you will never look at Ramen noodles or Duplex cookies the same again.

Not all meals are good on the inside. This is why some good old recipes are needed. *Fine Dining Prison Cookbook* and *Fine Dining Prison Cookbook 2* sure beat the chow hall. And for all of you "outsiders" who love them Ramen noodles, wait until you add a couple of chips and things and end up with a pizza, or even a full meal. You will simply be amazed at what you will discover within these pages.

There really is no end to what you will find as you flip through this book. You can be sure of one thing: a stove, oven, and refrigerator will not be needed. All the recipes are no-bake, nor do any need to be refrigerated. So, for all the college students, foodies, thrifty cooks, and any other curious person in the free world, go ahead and unhook the stove and unplug the microwave. You will not need either for these recipes.

In closing, I thank you for purchasing this book and for your support. Do not be afraid to substitute ingredients or to be creative. I truly hope and pray that each person who follows all the enclosed instructions enjoys what is produced as much as I liked producing it.

The first *Fine Dining Prison Cookbook* has an additional 150 recipes, as well as more inspiring quotes, tidbits of knowledge, food history, and much more, and can also be purchased through Freebird Publishers.

Yours truly,

Troy Neal Traylor, Sr.

Table of Contents

Acknowledgments v

Preface vii

Table of Contents 1

Supplies Needed – Inside/Outside 13

Helpful Cooking Tips 14

Section 1: Drinks 15

    Caramel Root Beer Float 16

    Classic Milkshake 17

    Hot Shot 18

    Ice Cream Float 19

    Mojo Tea 20

    Morning Pretty 21

    O-G Cadillac 22

    Protein Drink 23

    Remember Bennigan's 24

    Strawberry Margaritas 25

    Vanilla Mocha Coffee 26

    Yak Attack 27

Section 2: Dips & Cream Spreads 29

    Cheesy & Spicy Bean Dip 30

    Chocolate-Peanut Butter Cream Spread 31

    Crazy Spic-E Ketchup 32

    Cream Cheese Jalapeno Preserves 33

    Cream Cheese Spread 34

Guacamole 35

My French Onion Dip... 36

Ranch Dip Surprise.. 37

Salsa 38

Scrumptious Salsa... 39

Soy Sauce 40

Sweet & Spicy Salsa.. 41

Tartar Sauce... 42

Section 3: Side Dishes 43

Beef, Cheese, & Potatoes.. 44

Columbian Rice 45

Deviled Eggs 46

Down & Out Dirty Rice 47

Egg Salad 48

Home-Style Hash Browns... 49

Hot Jalapeno Bombers 50

Not Just Potatoes 51

Perfect Pickling.. 52

Poor Boy Sandwich 53

Side of Potatoes 54

Spanish Rice 55

Stuffed Jalapenos.. 56

Stuffed Pickles... 57

Sweet & Sour Rice... 58

Sweet & Sour Summer Sausage 59

Tahitian Rice... 60

Section 4: Soups & Chowders... 61

- Another Potato Soup 62
- Baltimore's Beef Stew 63
- Chicken Noodle Soup 64
- Cream of Tomato Soup 65
- Fish Gumbo 66
- Fish Stew 67
- Mackerel Chowder 68
- Meaty Gumbo 69
- Pork Stew 70
- Potato Soup 71
- Spicy Vegetable Soup 72
- Sweet & Sour Soup 73
- Tortilla Soup 74

Section 5: Beef Dishes 75
- Beef Facts & History 76
- Baltimore's Beef Pot Pie 80
- Beef & Dumplings 81
- Beef Tips & Rice 82
- Big Baller Burgers 83
- Cheeseburger Helper 84
- Cheese Steak Sandwich 85
- Chip and Cheese Burger 86
- Just Like Home Spaghetti 87
- Now That's Spaghetti 88
- Pot Roast Perfection 89
- Quick Snack 90
- Sheppard's Pie 91

Smothered Potatoes 92
Sweet Ole' Pot Roast 93
Tangy Summer Sausage & Rice 94

Section 6: Chicken Dishes 95
Poultry-Facts & History 96
BBQ Chicken 99
Cheesy Chicken Burritos 100
Chicken-Chili Nachos 101
Chicken & Dumplings 102
Chicken Salad 103
Chicken Spaghetti 104
Easy Baked Chicken 105
Lemon-Pepper Chicken 106
Orange Chicken with Sweet & Spicy Glaze 107
Sweet Chicken & Rice 109
Sweet & Sour Chicken & Rice 110
Tahitian Chicken 111

Section 7: Fish Dishes 113
Seafood Facts & History 114
BBQ Mackerel 117
Cellblock Cuisine 118
Fish Balls 119
Fish Boats 120
Fish Creole 121
Fish Salad 122
Fish Sticks 123
Jack Mack Fiesta 124

- Mackerel Casserole 125
- Mackerel Salad 126
- Salmon Dogs 127
- Salmon Salad 128
- Savory Paella 129
- Super-Seas Delight 130
- Sweet & Sour Mackerel 131
- Tahitian Mackerel 132
- Tahitian Tuna 133
- Thai Style Fish & Noodles 134
- Tuna Salad 135
- Tuna Wraps 136
- Zee Mack Patty #1 137
- Zee Mack Patty #2 138
- Zee Mack Patty #3 139

Section 8: Ham & Spam Dishes 141
- Pork Facts & History 142
- Fine Dining's Ham-Mac & Cheese 147
- Pineapple; Spam & Rice 148
- Spam Cheeseburgers 149
- Spam & Cheese Sandwich 150
- Spam Salad 151

Section 9: Mexican Dishes 153
- Fabulous Frito Pie 154
- Hearty Nachos 156
- Insider Burladas 157
- Killer Frito Pie 159

    Loaded and Coated Burritos 160

    Maryland Menudo 161

    My Gumbo 163

    My Menudo #1 164

    Nachos #1 165

    Nachos #2 166

    Tasty Tacos 167

    Tasty Tostitos 168

    Texas-Penn Tamales 169

    The Ultimate Burritos 170

Section 10: Pizzas 173

    Big House Spicy Pizza 174

    Hawaiian Pizza 175

    Meat Lover's Pizza 176

    Player's Pizza 177

    Slice of Seafood Pizza 179

Section 11: Breakfast 181

    Breakfast Burritos #1 182

    Breakfast Burritos #2 183

    Breakfast Burritos #3 184

    Breakfast Burritos #4 185

    Creamy Oatmeal 186

    My-Hop Pancakes 187

    More My-Hop Pancakes 188

    Peanut Butter Oatmeal 189

Section 12: Ad-Seg Delights 191

    Ad-Seg Goo-Losh 192

    Cheesy Chicken & Rice 193

    Chili Con Corn.. 194

    Good Ole Cabbage & Ham 195

    Greens & Ham 196

    Hungry Man Hobo 197

    Pork & Sauerkraut.. 198

    Seg-Soft Tacos 199

    Soup Salad 200

Section 13: Icings 201

    Peanut Butter Cream 202

    Strawberry or Raspberry Cream... 202

    Vanilla Cream 203

    Cinnamon, Butterscotch, & Lemon Icing 203

Section 14: Pie & Pie Crusts.. 205

    Chocolate Crust 206

    Sticky Sweet Pie Crust... 207

    Butter-Chocolate Cream Pie 208

    Chocolate Almond Cherry Pie 209

    Chocolate Malt Ball Pie 210

    Cinnamon Twist Crunch... 211

    Double Fudge Deluxe 213

    End of the Road 214

    Oatmeal Apple Pie 215

    Oatmeal Cream Pie.. 216

    One Sweet Chocolate Pie 217

    Raisin Nut Delight 219

    Reese's Pieces Pie 221

Snicker Doodle Delight 223

Sweet Potato Pie 224

Section 15: Cakes 225

Baltimore's Magic Trick 226

Chocolate Coconut Cake 227

Chocolate-Toffee Cake 228

Convict Cake 229

Dream Bar Cake 230

Gravitational Bliss 231

Mini Fruitcake 233

Peanut Butter & Jelly Cake 234

Simply a Chocolate Cake 235

Spice-E-Cake 236

Sweet Snickers Cake 237

Sweet Strawberry Cake 238

Texas Mudd 239

The Real Deal Cake 240

Too Die for Cake 242

Section 16: Cheesecakes 243

Cheesecake #1 244

Cheesecake #2 245

Big Red Apple Cheesecake 246

Cappuccino Crunch Cheesecake 247

Banana Nut Cheesecake 248

Cupcake Cheesecake 249

Ice Cream Cheesecake 250

Maple Syrup Cheesecake 251

Dr. Pepper Cheesecake 252

Strawberry Cheesecake 253

Strawberry Cheesecake #2 254

Root Beer Float Pie 255

Section 17: Candies & Treats 257

Armadillo Eggs 258

Baltimore's Butterscotch Brownies 259

Caramel Clusters 260

Chocolate Covered Marshmallow Treats 261

Chocolate Munchkins 262

Chocolate Popcorn Balls 263

Cream Filled Chocolate 264

Crunchy Chewy Granola 265

Coffee Delights 266

Dirty Mudslide 267

Min-choca Drops 268

One Sweet Treat 269

Oooie-Gooey & Chewy 270

Strawberry Dream Treats 271

Sweet Treat 2 272

Section 18: Bars of All Kinds 273

Baltimore's Best Bars 274

Bighouse Bars 275

Candy Bars 276

Cereal Bars 277

Mint Chocolate Bars 278

Section 19: Fudge 279

Baltimore's Fabulous Fudge 280

Butterfinger Delight Fudge 281

Section 20: Cookies 283

Candy Oatmeal Cookies 284

Chocolate Drop Sugar Cookies 285

Chocolate Oatmeal Cookies 286

Fudge Cookies 287

Peanut Butter Cookies 288

Section 21: Puddings 289

Chocolate Pudding 290

Banana Pudding 291

Lemon Pudding 292

Another Chocolate Pudding 293

Conversion Chart 294

Liquid Measurements 294

Dry Measurements 294

Shopping List 295

Bonus Section: A Few Secrets From the Outside 301

Avocado Deviled Eggs with Prosciutto Leaves 302

Baked Pancetta Baskets with Tomatoes, Crab, and Egg ... 303

Barbecue Chicken with Corn Bread Topper 304

Barley and Swiss Chard Skillet Casserole 305

Bone Broth-Braised Beef Short Ribs with Rosemary and Thyme 306

Candy Cane Cookie Bars 307

Cheddar Bacon Scallion Drop Biscuits 308

Crab Canapes Appetizer 309

Egg Cobb Tower with Grilled Chicken Breast 310

Frosted Cold-Brew Shortbread 311

Goat Cheese & Tomato Omelet 312

Greek Chicken & Spinach 313

Hot Chicken Sheet Pan Fajitas 314

Jalapeno and Caramelized Onion Mashed Potatoes 316

Lemon-Raspberry French Toast 317

Lentil Chili 318

Mango Smoothie 319

Olive Twists Appetizer 320

Pumpkin Spice Smoothie 321

Roasted Brussels Sprouts with Peppers 322

Roasted Vegetables with Tahini Dressing 323

Seasoned Pan-Seared Pork Tenderloin 324

Smoked Salmon Appetizers 325

Turkey and Pumpkin Skillet Lasagna 326

White Chocolate Pecan Ginger Bars 327

Hope

Hope looks for the good in people instead of harping on the worst.

Hope opens doors where despair closes them.

Hope discovers what can be done
instead of grumbling about what cannot.

Hope draws its clear power from a deep trust
in the basic goodness of human nature.

Hope "Lights a candle" instead of "cursing the darkness."

Hope regards problems, small or large, as opportunities.

Hope cherishes no illusions, nor does it yield to cynicism.

Hope sets big goals and is not frustrated
by repeated difficulties or setbacks.

Hope pushes ahead when it would be easy to quit.

Hope puts up with modest gains, realizing that
"the longest journey starts with one step."

Hope accepts misunderstandings as the price
for serving the greater good of others.

Hope is a good loser because it has
the divine assurance of final victory.

Supplies Needed – Inside/Outside

Inside	*Outside*
Large & Small Spread Bowls	Large & Small Mixing Bowls
12-ounce Coffee mug	Same
Insert Cup	16-ounce thick plastic cup
Hot Pot	Coffee Kettle
Empty Peanut Butter Jar	Same
Large and Small Chip Bags	Same
Rice bags	Same
Old Newspaper	Same
Crème Cookie Trays	Oreo Cookie Trays (3-row)
Plastic Trash Bags	Same
ID Card	Knife
Desire	Same
Patience	Same
Passion	Same
Appetite	Same
Commissary Spoon	Tablespoon and Teaspoon

Helpful Cooking Tips

Almost all of these recipes require a liquid of some sort to prepare. It is better if you begin with small amounts of the suggested liquid and slowly add as you go along. This is especially true in the preparation of the "sweets."

It is also helpful to know that drying times may vary depending on where you are, the time of year, and the brand names. Cheaper brands usually take longer.

When you are cooking in your hot pot, the best bags to use are rice bags. Chip bags can and will separate because of the heat. It is best to place a chip bag inside a second one if you must use chip bags. I refer to this as double bagging and will often direct you to "double bag." This will prevent your food from being flooded. Always submerge bags in water to heat. Hot pots are designed only for the heating of liquids.

Some food items, like instant rice and refried beans, require the addition of hot water. Often, not all of the water is absorbed and will need to be drained off after a certain amount of time has elapsed. In the book, this is referred to as "steeping." In cooking, to steep is to "soak (food) in water or other liquid so as to extract its flavor or to soften it." For our purposes, this should be done with the hottest water available.

Do not be afraid to add or subtract from these recipes. Each person has different tastes. Sizes of ingredients may vary slightly; they do not have to be exact. Try to adjust accordingly. (See Conversion Chart/Shopping List in the back of the book.)

If you are cooking in the free world and do not have a hot pot, the tastes may be a little different. Most likely, you will be surprised and appreciate our creativity.

Section 1:
Drinks

Caramel Root Beer Float

Ingredients
1 Milky Way candy bar
1 pint vanilla ice cream
1 (12 oz.) root beer soda

Directions
Cut the candy bar into small pieces and put them into an insert cup. Place insert into a hot pot and melt the candy bar. Grab two more insert cups and divide the ice cream between the two inserts. Pour half the melted candy bar over the ice cream and slowly add your root beer. Lightly stir. That's it, time to enjoy: Quick, fast, and easy.

*It's nice to be important,
but it's more important to be nice.*
– The Rock

Classic Milkshake

Ingredients
8 butterscotch candies (optional)
1 pint vanilla ice cream
1/4 coffee mug cold water
1 regular-size package M&M's (plain)
3/4 coffee mug instant milk

Directions
Crush candies into small pieces and set aside for a moment. In a large spread bowl, combine ice cream, instant milk, and water. Whip until you have a smooth and creamy mixture. Add candies to the mixture and stir well. Fill up your cup and drink up. Just like home!

*Speak when you are angry
and you will give the best speech you will ever regret.
– Ambrose Bierce.*

Troy Traylor

Hot Shot

Ingredients
3 pieces fireball candies
1 teaspoon sweetener or 2 tablespoons sugar
1 tablespoon favorite coffee
1 coffee mug hot water

Directions
Break up the fireball candies and put them in an insert cup. Add all the remaining ingredients, stir well, and place insert cup into a hot pot until all candies are melted. Stir well and drink up. Good, hot, and spicy.

*When angry, count to ten before you speak;
if very angry, a hundred.
– Thomas Jefferson*

Ice Cream Float

Ingredients
3/4 coffee mug instant milk
8 tablespoons hot water
1 pint vanilla ice cream
1 (12 oz.) Coca Cola

Directions
In a coffee mug, combine the instant milk with the hot water and stir until all is dissolved. You want it thick and creamy with no lumps. Add a little water if needed. Grab 2 insert cups and divide the ice cream between the two. Equally divide the milk mixture between insert cups and whip well. Once whipped, slowly add Coca-Cola and mix lightly. It's great on a hot day.

Life spent loving is a life well spent.
– Suzanne Clothier

Mojo Tea

Ingredients
8 fireball candies
1 coffee mug hot water
2 teaspoons lemon lime electrolytes or 6 tablespoons lemon Kool-Aid
7 tea bags
3 teaspoons sweetener or 6 tablespoons sugar

Directions
You will need 3 empty, 20 oz. water bottles. Crush all the fireball candies and place them in an insert cup. Add the seven tea Bags and the coffee mug, hot water to insert the cup, and stir. Place the insert cup in a hot pot and heat for 45 minutes. Remove from hot pot, squeeze out tea bags, and equally divide mixture between water bottles. Equally divide the sweetener/sugar and electrolyte between bottles and shake well. Once all is dissolved, top off bottles with cold water and shake again. Set bottles aside to cool down or pour over ice.

*He that keeps his mouth keeps his life:
but he that opens wide his lips shall have destruction.
– Proverbs 13:3*

Morning Pretty

Ingredients
12 pieces penny candy (different flavors)
4 butterscotch candies
1 tablespoon instant coffee
1 teaspoon sweetener or 2 tablespoons sugar
1 coffee mug hot water

Directions
Crush all candies into small pieces and place in an insert cup. Add the remaining ingredients and stir until all candies are melted. Place the insert cup into hot pot to speed up and keep hot. Once all the candies are melted, pour them into your coffee mug and enjoy. Great way to start any day!

For good or ill, your conversation is your advertisement. Every time you open your mouth, you let men look inside your mind.
– Bruce Burton

Troy Traylor

O-G Cadillac

Ingredients

1 tablespoon favorite coffee
2 teaspoons sweetener or 4 tablespoons sugar
4 tablespoons hot chocolate mix
1 coffee mug hot water
1 tablespoon creamer

Directions

In a coffee mug or insert cup, combine all the ingredients. Mix well and drink up. Sit back and sip, just like the O-Gs do it.

Hear no ill of a friend, nor speak any of an enemy.
– Benjamin Franklin

Protein Drink

Ingredients
1/3 coffee mug instant milk
3/4 coffee mug hot water
1 heaping tablespoon peanut butter
1/4 coffee mug instant oatmeal (any flavor)

Directions
Use an insert cup and combine instant milk and the hot water. Mix well. Now stir in peanut butter until completely melted. Add instant oatmeal, stir well, and drink up. This is great after a workout.

One man with courage is a majority.
— Andrew Jackson

Troy Traylor

Remember Bennigan's

Ingredients
2 teaspoons instant coffee
1 teaspoon sweetener or 2 tablespoons sugar
4 tablespoons Irish cream cappuccino
2 tablespoons chocolate syrup
1 coffee mug hot water

Directions
This is the easiest recipe ever: In your coffee mug or insert cup, combine all these ingredients and stir well. MMM! Drink up!

*A skillful man reads his dreams for self-knowledge,
yet not the details but the quality.
– Ralph Waldo Emerson*

Strawberry Margaritas

Ingredients
2 (12 oz.) strawberry sodas
16 tsps. lemon lime electrolyte or 32 tbsps. lemon Kool-Aid
92 oz. cold water (about 4 1/2 water bottles)

Directions
You will need 6 (20 oz.) empty water bottles. In a large spread bowl, combine sodas and electrolyte (or Kool-Aid) and mix until all electrolyte (or Kool-Aid) is dissolved. Equally divide the mixture between the water bottles and fill them the rest of the way with cold water. Lightly shake. Pour over ice and drink up. Not quite like home, but pretty close.

The best way to make your dreams come true is to wake up.
– Paul Valery

Troy Traylor

Vanilla Mocha Coffee

Ingredients
5 heaping tablespoons French vanilla creamer
1 teaspoon sweetener or 2 tablespoons sugar
1 heaping tablespoon instant coffee
1 coffee mug hot water

Directions
This one is very easy and very good. In an insert cup, combine all the ingredients and mix well. You can drink this hot or add ice and drink cold. Either way, it tastes great!

You must do the things you think you cannot do.
– Eleanor Roosevelt

Yak Attack

Ingredients
3/4 coffee mug instant coffee
12 tablespoons hot water
1 (12 oz.) Mountain Dew
1 (12 oz.) Code Red soda
1 (12 oz.) Cherry Coke or Cherry Pepsi

Directions
In your coffee mug, combine coffee and hot water. Stir until the coffee is melted into a thick syrup. The point of water is just to melt the coffee. Pour this syrup into a large spread bowl or a 2-quart container. Slowly, and I mean slowly, pour the sodas into the bowl/container as you stir. A foam will form as you add the sodas. Once all sodas are added, grab your cup. Fill your cup and slam the drink. Do not sip but slam. Keep filling the cup and keep slamming the drink until all is gone. The hairs on your head will stand tall. What a rush!

The question for each man to settle is not what he would do if he had means, time, influence, and educational advantages; the question is what he will do with the things he has. The moment a young man ceases to dream or to bemoan his lack of opportunities and resolutely looks his conditions in the face, and resolves to change them, he lays the cornerstone of solid and honorable success.
– Hamilton Wright Mabie

Helpful Cooking Tips

There is nothing more frustrating than over-salting a soup or stew you have spent countless hours – and countless dollars in ingredients – making. Try adding wedges of raw potato or apple to absorb the salt. Simmer for 10 minutes or so, then remove the wedges. If your soup is still too salty, sprinkle in a spoonful of sugar. If that doesn't work, a dash of apple-cider vinegar may do the trick. Finally, try diluting with water or low-sodium broth.

Turn Leftover Mashed Potatoes into Croquettes: Form cold mashed potatoes into little balls, dip in beaten egg, coat in breadcrumbs, and sauté or deep-fry. You can also mix in crabmeat or salmon.

Put Extra Rice to Good Use: If you've cooked more rice than you can eat, make rice pudding by adding butter, cinnamon, sugar, and milk. Or create fried rice by sautéing with a beaten egg, soy sauce, and sliced green onions. Or toss rice with slivered almonds and raisins for a Middle Eastern-inspired pilaf.

Save a Scorched Pan: To save a scorched pan, sprinkle the burned bottom with baking soda, then add four to five tablespoons salt, plus enough water to cover, and let stand overnight. Scrape out charred remains with a rubber spatula.

A solution of 1 tablespoon baking soda to 1-quart warm water will remove most "off" odors from plastic storage containers. Simply give them a thorough dip in the soda solution, rinse with fresh water, and dry.

Fresh fish will freeze well in a milk carton filled with water.

At your next party, chill your canned and bottled beverages by putting them in a top-load washer and covering them with ice. After you have removed all the drinks, just spin out the water.

Section 2:
Dips & Cream Spreads

Cheesy & Spicy Bean Dip

Ingredients
2 1/2 coffee mugs refried beans
4 coffee mugs hot water
2 (1.3 oz.) jalapeno peppers (singles)
1/4 (16 oz.) bottle squeeze cheese
2 tablespoons habanero sauce

Directions
In a large spread bowl, combine refried beans and hot water. Cover the bowl tightly and cook for 8 minutes. While waiting, dice jalapeno peppers. After the cook time has elapsed, add the remaining ingredients to the bowl and mix well. It is time to grab your favorite chips and an associate or two. Enjoy!

*Commitment leads to action.
Action brings your dream closer.
– Marcia Wieder*

Chocolate-Peanut Butter Cream Spread

Ingredients
3 tablespoons hot chocolate mix
1 tablespoon peanut butter (heaping)
2 (2 oz.) packages cream cheese
2 tablespoons hot water
1 (5.6 oz.) Maria cookies (or your favorite)

Directions
In a spread bowl, combine hot chocolate mix, peanut butter, cream cheese, and hot water. Mix thoroughly until smooth and creamy. Spread the mixture over the cookies and eat. Vanilla wafers are a nice substitute if Maria cookies are not available.

Wisdom is knowing what to do next, virtue is doing it.
– David Starr Jordan

Troy Traylor

Crazy Spic-E Ketchup

Ingredients
1/2 coffee mug ketchup
5 tablespoons mustard
3 tablespoons habanero sauce or chili garlic sauce
2 chili seasoning packets from Ramen noodles

Directions
In a small bowl or cup, combine all the ingredients and mix thoroughly. Put the mixture in a clean peanut butter jar. Eat with any of your favorite meals.

Commitment leads to action. Action brings your dreams closer.
– Marcia Wieder

Cream Cheese Jalapeno Preserves

Ingredients
4 (1.3 oz.) jalapeno peppers (singles)
2 (2 oz.) packages cream cheese
3/4 (12 oz.) bottle strawberry preserves
2 sleeves Golden Round crackers

Directions
In a small bowl, dice jalapeno peppers into tiny pieces. Do not remove the juice or the seeds. Add strawberry preserves to the bowl and mix well. Put all back into the bottle and set the bottle in a bowl of ice to stiffen. Open your crackers and put a splash of cream cheese and strawberry preserves on each one. Bet you can't eat just one!

I like the dreams of the future better than the history of the past.
– Patrick Henry

Troy Traylor

Cream Cheese Spread

Ingredients
1 (16 oz.) package Duplex cream cookies
8 (2 oz.) packages cream cheese
1/3 coffee mug instant milk
1/3 coffee mug hot chocolate mix
1/4 coffee mug hot water
1/2 (8 oz.) package Regal graham cookies

Directions
Separate the cream from the cookies and set the cookies aside. In a large spread bowl, combine the cream from cookies, cream cheese, instant milk, hot chocolate mix, and hot water. Whip until smooth and creamy. Now, crush the Regal Graham cookies and sprinkle over the top of the spread. Spoon cream cheese spread onto Duplex cookie halves and enjoy with a favorite drink.

Each person must live their life as a model for others.
– Rosa Parks

Guacamole

Ingredients

1 (6 oz.) bag salsa Verde chips
1 (1.3 oz.) jalapeno pepper (single)
3 tablespoons pickle juice
1 (1.375 oz.) package cheese and chive crackers
2 (2 oz.) packages of cream cheese
8 tablespoons squeeze cheese

Directions

Crush the chips and crackers into a fine powder. Dice the jalapeno pepper. Combine all the ingredients in a spread bowl and mix well. If it seems too dry for your taste, add a little more pickle juice and cream cheese. Enjoy this one with your favorite chips.

The end of wisdom is to dream high enough not to lose the dream in the seeking of it.
– William Faulkner

Troy Traylor

My French Onion Dip

Ingredients
2 (2 oz.) packages cream cheese
1 package chili Ramen seasoning
3 tablespoons pickle juice
1 packet beef Ramen seasoning
1 package chicken Ramen seasoning

Directions
You will use only 1/2 of the chili Ramen seasoning package and 1/2 of the chicken Ramen seasoning package. In a spread bowl, combine all the ingredients and mix well. If you desire a stronger taste, add a little more seasoning from leftover packages. Grab your favorite chips and dig in.

So often times it happens that we live our lives in chains.
And we never even know we have the key.
– Already Gone, by the Eagles, from the album
On the Border, 1974

Ranch Dip Surprise

Ingredients
1 (2 oz.) package of ranch dressing
2 tablespoons chili garlic sauce
3 tablespoons coffee creamer
1 package chili seasoning from Ramen

Directions
In a small bowl or cup, combine all the ingredients and thoroughly mix. This is great on chips and crackers of all kinds.

*It is hard to detect good luck;
it looks so much like something you earned.
– Frank A. Clark*

Salsa

Ingredients
2 (9 oz.) pickles (regular or hot)
3 tablespoons onion flakes
1 (12 oz.) V-8 juice
10 (1.3 oz.) jalapeno peppers (singles)
1 teaspoon garlic powder
1/2 (8 oz.) bottle habanera sauce

Directions
Cut up pickles and jalapeno peppers. In a large chip bag, combine all the ingredients and mix well. Double bag and place in a hot pot and heat for 4 hours. Once the cook time is complete, pour into a clean peanut butter jar. Allow to sit for 48 hours, shaking periodically, before using. You can also add a chili Ramen seasoning for a spicier salsa. This is great on meals, chips, and crackers.

All men dream but not equally. Those who dream by night in the dusty recesses of their minds wake in the day to find that it was vanity; but the dreamers of the day are dangerous men, for they may act their dream with open eyes to make it possible.
– T.E. Lawrence

Scrumptious Salsa

Ingredients
3 (1.3 oz.) jalapeno peppers (singles)
1/2 (2.75 oz.) bag pork skins (small)
1 package chili seasoning from Ramen
1 teaspoon black pepper
1 (9 oz.) dill pickle
1 (12 oz.) V-8 juice
2 tablespoons onion powder

Directions
Dice jalapeno peppers and pickle into small pieces. Crush pork skins into a fine powder. Using a large spread bowl, combine all ingredients and mix thoroughly. Pour the mixture into a clean peanut butter jar. Use on meals, chips, or snacks – simply scrumptious.

*Go confidently in the direction of your dreams.
Live the life you have imagined.
– Henry David Thoreau*

Soy Sauce

Ingredients
1 package beef Ramen seasoning
1/4 coffee mug hot water
1/4 teaspoon instant coffee (cheap coffee is best)

Directions
Combine all the ingredients in a coffee mug or small bowl and mix well. Make sure all is dissolved. You might need to adjust the recipe a little to suit your taste. This is great for meals and rice dishes. Not quite like home, but it works for where we are.

It takes a lot of courage to show someone else your dreams.
– Erma Bombeck

Fine Dining Prison Cookbook 2

Sweet & Spicy Salsa

Ingredients

1 (9 oz.) dill pickle
4 fireball candies
2 (1.3 oz.) jalapeno peppers (singles)
1 package spicy vegetable seasoning from Ramen

Directions

Slice the pickle and jalapeno peppers as you would for a burger. Crush fireball candies. Using an empty peanut butter jar, combine all the ingredients, including the pickle juice, and shake well. Allow to sit overnight before you begin to use. Shake occasionally.

Hope is the dream of the waking man.
– French Proverb

Tartar Sauce

Ingredients
1 (15 oz.) jar salad dressing (jar size may vary)
6 tablespoons pickle juice
1/2 (8 oz.) jar relish
1 teaspoon onion powder

Directions
In a large spread bowl, combine all the ingredients and mix well. Spoon the mixture back into the jar. You will have a little extra, so it's best to make it on the day of use, so there is no waste.

The best way to make your dreams come true is to wake up.
– Paul Valery

Section 3:
Side Dishes

Beef, Cheese, & Potatoes

Ingredients
1 (1.3 oz.) jalapeno pepper (single)
1 serving package beef & cheese sticks
1 1/2 coffee mugs four-cheese instant potatoes
3 coffee mugs hot water
1/4 package beef Ramen seasoning

Directions
Dice the jalapeno pepper, beef, and cheese into small pieces. In a large spread bowl, combine instant potatoes and hot water. Whip until smooth and creamy. You may need to adjust the amount of water for your desired taste. Once whipped, add the remaining ingredients and mix well. This makes a great side with your favorite meal.

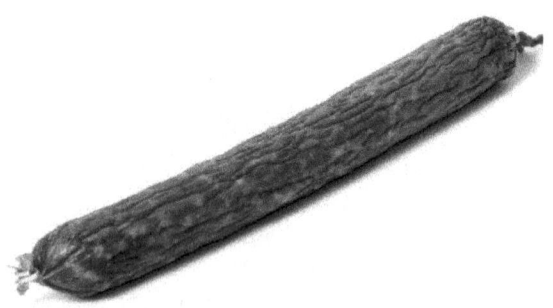

It is not what you look at that matters, it is what you see.
– Henry David Thoreau

Columbian Rice

Ingredients
1/4 (8 oz.) bag instant rice (white or brown)
1 (3 oz.) chili Ramen noodles
2 coffee mugs hot water
1 tablespoon salad dressing
1 (2 oz.) package ranch dressing
1 tablespoon soy sauce
2 (1.3 oz.) jalapeno peppers (singles)
1 (sleeve) package Saltine crackers

Directions
In a clean, large chip bag, combine rice, Ramen, and hot water. Double bag, tie up, and allow to cook for 8-10 minutes. Best to wrap in a towel while cooking. Once cooked, add salad dressing, ranch, and soy sauce. If you do not have soy sauce at your unit, a recipe for it can be found in this book. Dice your jalapeno peppers now and add to the bag. Mix well. Place the bag in a hot pot and cook for 1 hour. Once your meal is cooked, sprinkle on the seasoning from the Ramen. Put all in your spread bowl and dig in. You might want to invite an associate, unless you're really hungry. Eat on crackers.

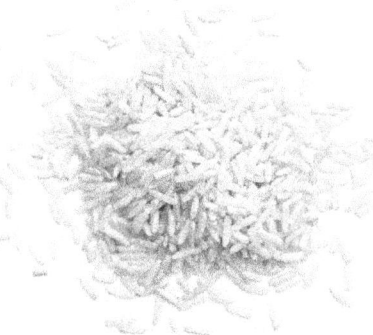

Dreams are the touchstones of our character.
– Henry David Thoreau

Troy Traylor

Deviled Eggs

Ingredients
6 hard-boiled eggs
1 teaspoon mustard
1 pinch pepper
1 tablespoon salad dressing
1 tablespoon relish
1 package chili Ramen seasoning

Directions
Peel and rinse the eggs. Cut in half and remove yokes. Use a small spread bowl and mash the yolks. Add salad dressing, mustard, relish, and pepper to the bowl and mix until well combined. Spoon the mixture back into the eggs and sprinkle with chili Ramen seasoning. Just like home!

Vision without action is a daydream.
Action without vision is a nightmare.
– Japanese Proverb

Down & Out Dirty Rice

Ingredients
1 (3.5 oz.) package mackerel
1 (5 oz.) summer sausage
1/4 (9 oz.) dill pickle
3 1/2 coffee mugs hot water
1/2 package chili Ramen seasoning
1 (11.25 oz.) package chili no beans
2 (1.3 oz.) jalapeno peppers (singles)
3/4 (8 oz.) bag instant rice (white or brown)
1 coffee mug jalapeno chips (crushed)
1 (2 oz.) package salted peanuts

Directions
You will need: 2 hot pots for this recipe. Drain juices from the mackerel and rinse off the chili package. Dice summer sausage. Add mackerel and summer sausage to the chili package and place in a hot pot to heat for 1 hour. While waiting, dice your jalapeno peppers and pickle. After 45 minutes, combine rice and hot water in a large spread bowl, cover tightly, and cook for 10 minutes. Drain any remaining water, crush chips, and add all remaining ingredients. Mix well. You can also add a bag of pork skins, as long as you hydrate them first.

A man may die, nations may rise and fall, but an idea lives on.
– John F. Kennedy

Egg Salad

Ingredients
6 hard-boiled eggs
3/4 tablespoon pickle juice
1 teaspoon pepper
1 teaspoon mustard
1/2 teaspoon garlic powder
1 tablespoon onion flakes
1 1/2 tablespoons salad dressing
1 tablespoon relish
1/4 teaspoon salt

Directions
Cut all the hard-boiled eggs into small pieces and put them in a large serving bowl. Use a couple of drops of hot water to hydrate the onion flakes. Now add all the ingredients to your bowl and mix well. Serve on bread, crackers, or tortilla chips.

When you cease to dream, you cease to live
– Malcom Forbes, American entrepreneur

Home-Style Hash Browns

Ingredients
5 (1.25 oz.) bags hot fries
1 (3 oz.) package Spam
1 1/2 tablespoons pickle juice
2 tablespoons refried beans
1/4 (3 oz.) chili Ramen noodles
1/3 coffee mug hot water
1/4 package chili Ramen seasoning
ketchup, hot sauce, and squeeze cheese to taste

Directions
Crush hot fries lightly and finely dice Spam. In a large spread bowl, combine hot fries, Spam, pickle juice, refried beans, Ramen, seasoning, and hot water. Mix well. Put this mixture in a clean chip bag, double bag, and place in a hot pot to heat for 1 1/2 hours. When finished, put hash browns in your spread bowl and top off with ketchup, hot sauce, and cheese. Just like home, right?

The truth that makes men free is for the most part the truth which men prefer not to hear.
– Herbert Agar

Troy Traylor

Hot Jalapeno Bombers

Ingredients
10 (1.3 oz.) jalapeno peppers (singles)
1/4 (8 oz.) bag instant white rice
1 1/4 coffee mugs hot water
1 (8 oz.) package Mexican beef
2 packages chili Ramen seasoning
2 (2 oz.) packages cream cheese
1/4 coffee mug salsa
2 handfuls jalapeno chips
2 handfuls corn chips

Directions
Cut stems out of jalapeno peppers and clean out the seeds. (*Note*: To clean out seeds and stem from jalapeno peppers, cut off the top of the pepper and use a spoon handle to clean out the insides.) Set the peppers aside. In a spread bowl, combine the rice and hot water, cover tightly, and steep for 10 minutes. Drain any remaining water. Add Mexican beef, Ramen seasonings, 1 1/2 packages cream cheese, and salsa to the bowl, and mix well. Crush the jalapeno chips, add to the bowl, and mix again. Carefully fill the jalapeno peppers with this mixture. Once all are filled, crush the corn chips into a fine powder. With the remaining cream cheese, coat each pepper and roll the peppers in crushed corn chips to coat. Carefully place peppers into a clean rice bag and place the bag into a hot pot to heat for 2 full hours. These are both juicy as well as delicious.

A positive attitude may not solve all your problems, but it will annoy enough people to make it worth the effort.
– Herm Albright

Fine Dining Prison Cookbook 2

Not Just Potatoes

Ingredients
1 (5 oz.) summer sausage
1 1/2 coffee mugs of your favorite instant potatoes
3 coffee mugs hot water
1 (2 oz.) package cream cheese
1 tablespoon onion flakes
1/2 teaspoon garlic powder
1 (1.375 oz.) package cheese and chive crackers

Directions
Cut up summer sausage into tiny pieces. In a large spread bowl, combine instant potatoes and hot water. Whip until smooth and creamy. Adjust the water for your desired consistency. Now stir in summer sausage, cream cheese, and seasonings. Crush crackers and top off. Lightly stir. Very good.

Truth is a fruit that should not be plucked until it is ripe.
– Voltaire

Perfect Pickling

Ingredients
1 (9 oz.) dill pickle
1 1/2 teaspoons lemon lime electrolyte or 4 tablespoons Kool-Aid
3 (1.3 oz.) jalapeno pepper (singles)

Directions
Slice the pickle as you would for a burger and dice the jalapeno peppers. Grab an empty peanut butter jar. Pour the pickle juice into the peanut butter jar, add the electrolyte or Kool-Aid, and stir until everything is dissolved. Now add the pickle slices and jalapeno pepper pieces to the jar. Shake and allow to steep for 3 days before using. Shake from time to time to mix ingredients. It really brings burgers and meals to life.

The high-minded man must care more for the truth than for what people think.
– Aristotle (384-322 B.C.)

Poor Boy Sandwich

Ingredients
1/4 (9 oz.) dill pickle
2 slices bread
3 tablespoons squeeze cheese
1 (1.3 oz.) jalapeno pepper (single)
1 good tablespoon sandwich spread

Directions
Slice the pickle and jalapeno pepper as you would for a burger. Place all on a slice of bread and top with cheese, sandwich spread, and the remaining piece of bread. That's how we poor boys do it. Sliced cheese is just as good.

Do not wait for leaders; do it alone, person to person.
– St. Teresa of Calcutta

Side of Potatoes

Ingredients
1 (5 oz.) summer sausage
2 (1.375 oz.) packages cheese and chive crackers
1 1/2 coffee mugs of your favorite instant potatoes
3 coffee mugs hot water
2 tablespoons squeeze cheese
1 (1.3 oz.) jalapeno pepper (single)

Directions
Dice the summer sausage into fairly small pieces and crush the crackers. Using a large spread bowl, combine the instant potatoes and hot water. Whip until smooth and creamy. Adjust the water for your desired consistency. Dice the pepper, add the rest of the listed ingredients, and mix well. If you have butter available, a tablespoon or two is a nice touch. Again, may need to add a few tablespoons of water, depending on the name brand.

Freedom comes from knowing the truth; bondage comes from missing it.
– Charles Stanley

Spanish Rice

Ingredients
1 (12 oz.) V-8 juice
1 (8 oz.) package Mexican beef
1 teaspoon onion powder
1/4 (8 oz.) bag white or brown instant rice
1 (4 oz.) serving corn from tray
6 tablespoons salsa

Directions
Combine all the ingredients except the salsa in a large, clean chip bag, double bag, and place in a hot pot to heat for 1 1/2 hours. When done, pour everything into your spread bowl, add the salsa, and mix well. Nice little dish.

*The truth isn't always beauty,
but the hunger for it is.
– Nadine Gordimer*

Troy Traylor

Stuffed Jalapenos

Ingredients
20 (1.3 oz.) jalapeno peppers (singles)
1 (11.25 oz.) package chili no beans
1 (8 oz.) package Mexican ground beef
1 coffee mug refried beans
2 1/4 coffee mugs of hot water
1 coffee mug crushed jalapeno chips
4 (2 oz.) packages cream cheese
1/4 (16 oz.) bottle squeeze cheese
1/2 coffee mug crushed party mix

Directions
Cut the jalapeno peppers in half, lengthwise, and clean out the seeds. Rinse off both meat packages and place them in a hot pot to heat. While waiting, combine refried beans and hot water in a spread bowl. Cover tightly and steep for 8 minutes. Once the meat packages are hot, add them to the refried beans. Now, crush jalapeno chips and add chips, cream cheese, and squeeze cheese to the bowl and thoroughly mix. Use this mixture to fill pepper halves. Crush the party mix and top each. Any leftover mixture can be used with nacho chips or tortilla chips. Trust that every bite is simply delicious.

Courage is what it takes to stand up and speak, courage is also what it takes to sit down and listen.
– Winston Churchill

Fine Dining Prison Cookbook 2

Stuffed Pickles

Ingredients
4 (9 oz.) pickles (regular or hot)
1 (4.23 oz.) package tuna
1 package chili Ramen seasoning
3 tablespoons pickle juice
1/4 tablespoon mustard
1 teaspoon sweetener or 2 tablespoons sugar
1/2 (14 oz.) bottle salad dressing
hot sauce of choice to taste
1/4 (6 oz.) bag Salsa Verde chips
1/4 (2.75 oz.) bag pork skins
1/4 (8 oz.) bag jalapeno chips
1 (1.25 oz.) bag hot fries

Directions
Cut pickles in half, lengthwise, and clean out the seeds. Set jalapeno chips and hot fries aside. Crush remaining chips and combine all the rest of the ingredients in a large spread bowl and mix well. Let this mixture sit for 30 minutes. Now, crush the jalapeno chips and hot fries and add them to the mixture. Mix well. Use this mixture to fill pickle halves. If you have cheese puffs, crush a handful and top pickles. Any leftover mixture can be used with nachos or tortilla chips. Wash all down with your favorite drink.

Men occasionally stumble over the truth, but most of them pick themselves up and hurry off as if nothing ever happened.
– Winston Churchill

Sweet & Sour Rice

Ingredients
1/2 (8 oz.) bag instant white rice
4 tablespoons pickle juice
1 (12 oz.) pineapple orange juice
2 teaspoons sweetener or 4 tablespoons sugar

Directions
In a large clean chip bag, combine rice, pineapple, and orange juice. Double bag and tie closed. Place the bag in a hot pot to heat for 1 1/2 hours. You may need to add a little water as this is heating to keep it moist. Once the cook time is up, remove from the hot pot, drain any excess liquids, and place all in a spread bowl. Now add the pickle juice and sweeteners or sugar. Mix well. Serve with your favorite meal. You can add fruit to this once it's cooked, if you desire.

Truth is stranger than fiction, but it is because fiction is obliged to stick to the possibilities; truth isn't.
– Mark Twain (1835-1910)

Sweet & Sour Summer Sausage

Ingredients

6 tablespoons pickle juice
1/2 tablespoon cheap coffee
2 (4 oz.) lemon pies
2 1/4 coffee mugs hot water
2 (2.75 oz.) bag pork skins
2 packages beef Ramen seasoning
1 (5 oz.) summer sausage
1/2 (8 oz.) bag instant white rice
1 teaspoon orange electrolyte or 2 tablespoons Kool-Aid

Directions

Use an insert cup and combine pickle juice, beef seasoning packages, and coffee. Stir until all is dissolved. Place the insert cup into a hot pot to heat for 30 minutes. While waiting, dice the summer sausage into small pieces. Now, combine ingredients from the insert cup with the summer sausage in a larger clean chip bag. Double bag and place the bag in a hot pot to heat for 30 minutes. While this is heating, combine rice, hot water, and electrolyte or Kool-Aid in a large spread bowl. Cover tightly and steep for 10 minutes. While waiting, remove the lemon filling from the pies and add it to the summer sausage bag. Once all cook time is up, drain any excess liquid from the rice bowl. Lightly crush pork skins and combine all ingredients in one bowl. Stir well. Let it sit for 5 minutes before you eat. You might want to invite an associate, unless you are really hungry.

> *If you have an hour, will you not improve that hour, instead of idling it away?*
> *– Lord Chesterfield*

Troy Traylor

Tahitian Rice

Ingredients
1/3 onion (sub 3 tablespoons onion flakes)
2 tablespoons homemade soy sauce
1/4 coffee mug of butter
1 1/2 tablespoons mustard
1/4 coffee mug brown sugar
1 1/2 tablespoons cornstarch
3/4 package chicken Ramen seasoning
1 (4 oz.) serving fruit cocktail or pineapple
1 coffee mug instant white rice
1 (12 oz.) can of any type of fruit juice
1/4 coffee mug hot water
1 teaspoon black pepper
1 (2 oz.) package energy mix or salted peanuts, set aside.

Directions
You will need a little help from the kitchen for this recipe. Dice the onion and mix with the homemade soy sauce (see recipe in this book). Use a clean, large chip bag and combine all these ingredients, and mix well. Double bag and place in a hot pot to heat for 3 1/2 hours. You may need to add a little water to keep it moist while cooking. Stir occasionally. Once the cook time elapses, drain any remaining liquid and put the mixture in a spread bowl. Top with the energy mix or peanuts and enjoy. This is a great dish to eat with any fish dish. Anyway you eat it, you will love it. Most Tahitian dishes call for the dish to be marinated; this dish does not.

It is not until you become a parent that your judgement slowly turns to compassion and understanding.
– Erma Bombeck

Section 4:
Soups & Chowders

Troy Traylor

Another Potato Soup

Ingredients
3 coffee mugs instant potato flakes (any flavor)
2 hot pots of hot water
2 (1.3 oz.) jalapeno peppers (singles)
1 (5 oz.) summer sausage
1 teaspoon black pepper
3 (2 oz.) packages cream cheese
3/4 coffee mug instant milk
3 tablespoons squeeze cheese
1/2 (8 oz.) bag jalapeno chips

Directions
In a large spread bowl, combine potato flakes and all the hot water. Mix this well. You want it thick like a chowder with all the lumps and clumps gone. Add water if needed to get the chowder to the right consistency. Finely dice jalapeno peppers and summer sausage. Add these to your bowl and stir well. Combine all the remaining ingredients, except for the jalapeno chips, and mix well. Add any water needed to maintain a chowder consistency. Bag and cook in a hot pot for 3 hours. It is best to use two hot pots and split the soup equally. Double bag to avoid flooding. Stir occasionally and thin with water as needed. Add jalapeno chips, whole, to the bag(s). Lightly stir and heat for another hour, stirring occasionally. Then it's time to fill up the bowl and dig in. Feeds two hungry people.

> *Dost thou love life? Then do not squander time,*
> *for that is the stuff life is made of.*
> *– Benjamin Franklin*

Baltimore's Beef Stew

Ingredients
3 tablespoons corn starch (if available)
1 (4 oz.) serving green beans (from tray)
1 (8 oz.) serving ground beef (from tray)
1 (4 oz.) serving of corn (from tray)
1 (4 oz.) serving carrots (from tray)
1 (8 oz.) package beef tips
1 heaping tablespoon onion flakes
2 tablespoons of instant milk
2 packages beef Ramen seasoning
2 coffee mugs hot water

Directions
If starch is available, whip it with a few drops of water until all of the chunks are gone. Using a large chip bag, combine all the ingredients and mix well. Double bag and place in a hot pot to heat for 3 to 4 hours. Stir occasionally. Once ready, fill your bowl and enjoy. Buttered rice or instant potatoes are a nice side dish with this meal.

Carpe Diem (Latin adage: Seize the day)

Chicken Noodle Soup

Ingredients

2 tablespoons corn starch (if available)
1 (7 oz.) package chicken chunks
1 (1.3 oz.) jalapeno pepper (single)
1 package chicken Ramen seasoning
1 (4 oz.) serving carrots
1 (3 oz.) chicken Ramen noodles (not crushed)
3 coffee mugs hot water
3 tablespoons squeeze cheese
4 heaping tablespoons instant milk

Directions

If starch is available, whip with a few drops of water until all the chunks are gone. Dice jalapeno pepper. Using a large chip bag, combine all ingredients and mix well. Double bag and place in a hot pot to heat for 3 to 4 hours. Stir occasionally. Nice treat if you're a little under the weather. Butter and saltine crackers are a nice addition.

A prison made of pearls and gold is still a prison.
— Philippine proverb

Cream of Tomato Soup

Ingredients
1 1/2 coffee mugs ketchup
3/4 coffee mug instant milk
1/2 teaspoon salt
1 coffee mug hot water
1 tablespoon black pepper

Directions
In a clean, large chip bag, combine all ingredients, mix well, and place in a hot pot to heat for 3 hours. Stir occasionally. It is best to double the bag. You may need to add a little water as you cook to get your preferred consistency. This is a great dish on a cold day. Saltine crackers and butter go great with this soup.

One today is worth two tomorrows.
– Benjamin Franklin

Fish Gumbo

Ingredients:

1 (9 oz.) pickle
3 (12 oz.) V-8 juice
2 (4.6 oz.) packages red beans and rice
2 (3.5 oz.) packages mackerel
1 (3.53 oz.) package tuna with jalapeno peppers
1 (5.6 oz.) package pink salmon
1 coffee mug hot water
1 (10 oz.) package flour tortillas

Directions

Dice pickle. Heat the V-8 juices as hot as possible. Once heated, combine all the remaining ingredients in a large chip bag and mix well. Wrap in a towel and allow to cook for 20 minutes. Once cooked, unwrap the bean mixture and spoon onto flour tortillas. Roll up and enjoy with your favorite chips and drink. You do not need to drain these meat packages.

There is more to life than simply increasing its speed.
– Mahatma Gandhi

Fish Stew

Ingredients
3 (3.5 oz.) packages mackerel
1 (11.25 oz.) package beef stew
2 packages chili Ramen seasoning
2 (1.3 oz.) jalapeno peppers (singles)
1 (5 oz.) summer sausage
1/2 (8 oz.) bag instant white rice
2 flour tortillas
1 (12 oz.) V-8 juice
2 tablespoons hot sauce of choice
1 package beef Ramen seasoning
1/2 (9 oz.) dill pickle
1 (3 oz.) beef Ramen noodles
2 coffee mugs hot water
3 tablespoons squeeze cheese

Directions
In a coffee mug or small bowl, drain the juices from the mackerel. In a large chip bag, combine the mackerel juice, V-8, beef stew package, hot sauce, and all three seasoning packages. Finely dice jalapeno peppers, pickle, and summer sausage, add to the bag, and mix well. Double bag, tie off, and heat in a hot pot for 1 1/2 hours. Stir occasionally. After an hour and 20 minutes, in a large spread bowl, combine mackerel, Ramen noodles, rice, and hot water. Cover bowl tightly. Tear up flour tortillas into pieces. Drain all water from the spread bowl and pour the bag over the top. Add flour tortilla pieces and mix well. Top off with cheese and lightly stir.

There is no saint without a past and no sinner without a future.
– Pope Francis

Troy Traylor

Mackerel Chowder

Ingredients
1 (1.3 oz.) jalapeno pepper (single)
1 (3.5 oz.) package mackerel
8 tablespoons instant milk
2 (2 oz.) packages cream cheese
1 (3 oz.) chicken Ramen noodles & seasoning package
1 1/2 coffee mugs hot water

Directions
Dice the jalapeno pepper and put it in a large chip bag. Add all the rest of these ingredients together and mix well. Double bag and place in a hot pot to heat for 2 hours. You may have to add a little water as you heat to maintain a chowder consistency. If you add water, add a little more instant milk as well. This one is a nice change.

Make each day your masterpiece.
– John Wooden

Meaty Gumbo

Ingredients
1 (4 oz.) package turkey bites
1 (5 oz.) summer sausage
2 (1.3 oz.) jalapeno peppers (singles)
1 (7 oz.) chicken chunks
2 (4.6 oz.) packages red beans and rice
2 (12 oz.) V-8 juice
1 coffee mug hot water
1 (10 oz.) package flour tortilla

Directions
Dice the turkey bites, summer sausage, and jalapeno peppers. Heat both cans of V-8 juice as hot as possible. Now, in a large chip bag, combine all the ingredients except the flour tortillas. Mix well, wrap in a towel, and allow this to cook for 20 minutes. Afterward, unwrap the bean mixture and roll into flour tortillas. This is an incredibly delicious meal. You can top it with cheese, but it really doesn't need it.

The worst of all tragedies is not to die young, but to live until I am 75 and not yet ever truly lived.
– Martin Luther King Jr.

Troy Traylor

Pork Stew

Ingredients
2 (3 oz.) packages of Spam
2 tablespoons onion flakes
1 (4 oz.) serving of corn, if available
1 package shrimp Ramen seasoning
1 (2.75 oz.) bag pork skins
1/2 teaspoon garlic powder
1 (4 oz.) serving green beans, if available
2 coffee mugs hot water

Directions
Dice Spam into fairly small pieces. Lightly crush pork skins. Using a clean, large chip bag, combine all the ingredients and mix well. Double bag and place in a hot pot to heat for 3 to 4 hours. Stir occasionally. You can add a shot of squeeze cheese to this, but you really do not need to. It's great with a side of instant potatoes.

The summer night is like perfection of thought.
– Wallace Stevens

Potato Soup

Ingredients
3 coffee mugs of instant potato flakes (any flavor)
2 hot pots of hot water
1 (2.75 oz.) bag pork skins
1 (1.375 oz.) package cheese and chive crackers
3/4 coffee mug instant milk
4 tablespoons squeeze cheese
2 (2 oz.) packages cream cheese

Directions
In a large spread bowl, combine potato flakes and all the hot water. Mix this well. Want thick like chowder and all the lumps and clumps gone. Add water if needed to get chowder consistency. Crush pork skins and crackers. Now add all remaining ingredients to the bowl and thoroughly mix. You want to bag this up in a large chip bag and cook in a hot pot for 3 hours. It is best to use two hot pots and split the soup equally. Double your bag to avoid flooding. Stir occasionally and thin with water as needed. This will feed two hungry people.

Time is really the only capital that any human being has, and the one thing that he can't afford to lose.
–Thomas A. Edison (1847-1931)

Spicy Vegetable Soup

Ingredients
1 (4 oz.) serving corn, if available
1 (4 oz.) serving green beans, if available
1 (4 oz.) serving carrots, if available
1 teaspoon black pepper
1 tablespoon hot sauce of choice
1 package chili Ramen seasoning
2 coffee mugs of hot water
1/2 teaspoon garlic powder
1 tablespoon onion flakes

Directions
In a clean, large chip bag, combine all the ingredients, mix well, and place in a hot pot to heat for 6 hours. It is best to double the bag. This is great on a cold day or for a runny nose.

Time is free, but it is priceless. You can't own it, but you can use it. You can't keep it, but you can spend it. Once you've lost it, you can never get it back.
  – Harvey Mackay

Sweet & Sour Soup

Ingredients

2 coffee mugs hot water
3 teaspoons sweetener or 6 tablespoons sugar
12 tablespoons of pickle juice
2 (4 oz.) servings carrots, if available
1 heaping teaspoon black pepper
8 tablespoons instant milk

Directions

In a clean chip bag, combine all the ingredients, mix well, and place in a hot pot to heat for 4 hours. It is best to double the bag. This is great for a sore throat: a new idea as well as a new taste! Buttered crackers go great with this soup.

Sometimes you just have to give yourself what you wish someone else would give you.
– Dr. Phil

Troy Traylor

Tortilla Soup

Ingredients
2 (3 oz.) beef Ramen noodles
1 (8 oz.) package Mexican beef
1/4 (16 oz.) bottle of squeeze cheese
1/2 (16 oz.) bag tortilla chips
5 coffee mugs hot water
1 package beef Ramen seasoning
2 tablespoons habanero sauce

Directions
Cook Ramen in a large spread bowl using all 5 coffee mugs of hot water. Rinse off the meat package and place it in a hot pot to heat. Once the meat package is hot, add it to the Ramen and stir well. Now add beef seasoning and squeeze cheese. Mix thoroughly. Add your tortilla chips now and allow them to soften. Top off with habanero sauce and lightly mix. Get comfortable and enjoy your meal.

A single day is enough to make us a little larger, or another time, a little smaller.
– Paul Klee

Section 5:
Beef Dishes

Beef Facts & History

Wikipedia

The word beef is from the Latin *bōs*, in contrast to cow, which is from the Middle English *cou* (both words have the same Indo-European root *g^wou-). After the Norman Conquest, the French-speaking nobles who ruled England naturally used French words to refer to the meats they were served. Thus, various Anglo-Saxon words were used for the animal (such as *nēat*, or *cu* for adult females) by the peasants, but the meat was called *boef* (ox) (Modern French *boeuf*) by the French nobles – who did not often deal with the live animal – when it was served to them. This is one example of the common English dichotomy between the words for animals (with largely Germanic origins) and their meat (with Romanic origins) that is also found in such English word-pairs as pig/pork, deer/venison, sheep/mutton, and chicken/poultry. Beef is cognate with bovine through the Late Latin *bovīnus*.

Beef is the culinary name for meat from cattle, particularly skeletal muscle. Humans have been eating beef since prehistoric times. Beef is a source of high-quality protein and nutrients.

Beef skeletal muscle meat can be used as is by merely cutting into certain parts, such as roasts, short ribs, or steak (filet mignon, sirloin steak, rump steak, rib steak, rib eye steak, hanger steak, etc.), while other cuts are processed (corned beef or beef jerky). Trimmings, on the other hand, are usually mixed with meat from older, leaner (therefore tougher) cattle, are ground, minced, or used in sausages. The blood is used in some varieties called blood sausage. Other parts that are eaten include other muscles and offal, such as the oxtail, liver, tongue, tripe from the reticulum or rumen, glands (particularly the pancreas and thymus, referred to as sweetbread), the heart, the brain (although forbidden where there is a danger of bovine spongiform encephalopathy, BSE, commonly called Mad Cow disease, the kidneys, and the tender testicles of the bull (known in the United States as prairie oysters, or Rocky Mountain oysters). Some intestines are left as is, but are more often cleaned and used as a natural sausage casing for making beef stock.

Beef from steers and heifers is similar. Depending on economics, the number of heifers kept for breeding varies. The meat from older bulls, because it is usually tougher, is frequently used for mince (known as ground beef in the United States). Cattle raised for beef may be allowed to roam free on grasslands, or may be confined at some stage in pens as part of a large feeding operation called a feedlot (or concentrated animal feeding operation), where they are usually fed a ration of grain, protein, roughage, and a vitamin/mineral pre-blend.

Beef is the third most widely consumed meat in the world, accounting for about 25% of meat production worldwide, after pork and poultry at 38% and 30% respectively. In absolute numbers, the United States, Brazil, and the People's Republic of China are the world's three largest consumers of beef; Uruguay, however, has the highest beef and veal consumption per capita, followed by Argentina and Brazil. According to the data from OECD, the average Uruguayan ate over 42 kg (93 lbs.) of beef or veal in 2014, representing the highest beef/veal consumption per capita in the world. In comparison, the average Americans consumed only about 24 kg (53 lb.) of beef or veal in the same year, while African Countries, such as Mozambique, Ghana, and Nigeria, consumed the least beef or veal per capita.

Cows are considered sacred in Hinduism, and most observant Hindus who do eat meat almost always abstain from beef.

In 2015, the world's largest exporters of beef were India, Brazil, and Australia. Beef production is also important to the economies of Uruguay, Canada, Paraguay, Mexico, Argentina, Belarus, and Nicaragua.

History

People have eaten the flesh of bovines from prehistoric times; some of the earliest known cave paintings, such as those of Lascaux, show aurochs in hunting scenes. People domesticated cattle around 8,000 BC to provide ready access to beef, milk, and leather. Most cattle originated in the Old World, with the exception of bison hybrids, which originated in the Americas. Examples include the Wagyu from Japan, Ankole-Watusi from Egypt, and longhorn Zebu from the Indian subcontinent.

It is unknown exactly when people started cooking beef. Cattle were widely used across the Old World as draft animals (oxen), for milk, or specifically for human consumption. With the mechanization of farming, some breeds were specifically bred to increase meat yield, resulting in Chianina and Charolais cattle, or to improve the texture of meat, giving rise to the Murray Grey, Angus, and Wagyu. Some breeds have been selected for both meat and milk production, such as the Brown Swiss (Braunvieh).

In the United States, the growth of the beef business was largely due to expansion in the Southwest. Upon the acquisition of grasslands through the Mexican American War of 1848, and later the expulsion of the Plains Indians from this region and the Midwest, the American livestock industry began, starting primarily with the taming of wild longhorn cattle. Chicago and New York City were the first to benefit from these developments in their stockyards and in their meat markets.

Beef cattle are raised and fed using a variety of methods, including feedlots, free range, ranching, backgrounding, and intensive animal farming.

Cuts

Beef is first divided into primal cuts, pieces of meat initially separated from the carcass during butchering. These are basic sections from which steaks and other subdivisions are cut. The term "primal cut" is quite different from "prime cut," used to characterize cuts considered to be of higher quality. Since the animal's legs and neck muscles do the most work, they are the toughest; the meat becomes more tender as the distance from

the hoof and horn increases. Different countries and cuisines have
different cuts and names, and sometimes use the same name for a different cut; for example, the cut described as "brisket" in the United States is from a significantly different part of the carcass than British brisket.

Troy Traylor

Baltimore's Beef Pot Pie

Ingredients
2 (8 oz.) servings ground beef from tray
1 (4 .oz.) serving green beans from tray
1 (4 oz.) serving carrots from tray
1 (11.25 oz.) package BBQ beef
1 (16 oz.) bag vanilla wafers
8 flour tortillas
3 tablespoons squeeze cheese
1 teaspoon onion powder
1/2 teaspoon garlic powder
6 tablespoons hot water
1 package beef Ramen seasoning
1 teaspoon onion flakes

Directions
Crush the vanilla wafers into a fine powder and place 2/3 of the bag into a large spread bowl. Spoon enough water into this bowl to knead into a moist, but not wet, dough (approximately 3-3 1/2 tablespoons). Work this dough into a pie crust and smooth out. Cover the dough with 4 tortillas and set aside. In a second spread bowl wet the rest of the wafers with approximately 2 tablespoons of water and knead into a moist dough. Flatten this one out into the bottom of the spread bowl with a small lip and set aside. Using a clean chip bag, combine all ingredients except the remaining four flour tortillas and mix well. Double bag and place in a hot pot to cook for 2 hours. Stir occasionally. Once cooked, pour the mixture into the pie crust. Cover with the remaining 4 flour tortillas and the remaining dough. Pinch around the bowl rim to seal. Let sit for 15 minutes and dig in. Takes a little work for this delicious meal.

Begin now to be what you will be hereafter.
– Saint Jerome

Fine Dining Prison Cookbook 2

Beef & Dumplings

Ingredients
1 (11.25 oz.) package BBQ beef
2 (8 oz.) packages beef tips in gravy
1 (12 oz.) V-8 juice
1 (3 oz.) beef Ramen noodles (not crushed)
1 (4 oz.) serving green beans from tray
1 (4 oz.) serving carrots from tray
1 package beef Ramen seasoning
1 tablespoon onion flakes
1/2 coffee mug hot water
1/2 teaspoon garlic powder
6 flour tortillas

Directions
Open the BBQ beef package and remove all beef pieces. Set the BBQ sauce aside. In a large clean chip bag, combine all ingredients, except the flour tortillas, and mix well. Double bag and place in a hot pot to heat for 2 hours. Right before this cook time is up,
tear the flour tortillas into 4 pieces each. Roll these pieces into a ball and add them to the bag. Place the bag back into the hot pot for an additional 1 1/2 hours. If you do not want to waste the BBQ sauce, make up a serving of instant potatoes, and pour BBQ sauce over the top. What an awesome meal this is.

It's never too late to be what you might have been.
– George Eliot

Beef Tips & Rice

Ingredients

2 (1.3 oz.) jalapeno peppers (singles)
1 (8 oz.) package beef tips
1/2 (8 oz.) bag instant white rice
1 package beef Ramen seasoning
4 tablespoons squeeze cheese
1 teaspoon garlic powder
1/2 teaspoon coriander and annatto
1 coffee mug hot water
2 tablespoons BBQ sauce
1 tablespoon butter

Directions

Cut jalapeno peppers into small pieces and put them in a large, clean chip bag. Set butter aside and add all remaining ingredients to the bag and mix well. Double bag and place in a hot pot to heat for 3 hours. Do not let it dry out. You might need to add a little water as it heats. Stir occasionally. Once cooked, pour the mixture into a large spread bowl, add butter, stir well, and enjoy. This is a great meal with buttered bread or saltine crackers.

Time is the coin of your life. It is the only coin you have, and only you can determine how it will be spent. Be careful lest you let other people spend it for you.
– Carl Sandburg, poet and author, 1878-1967

Big Baller Burgers

Ingredients
2 (11.25 oz.) packages BBQ beef
5 (1.3 oz.) jalapeno peppers (singles)
1 (8 oz.) bag jalapeno chips
2 (9 oz.) pickles
1 loaf bread
squeeze cheese, hot sauce, and salad dressing to taste

Directions
Rinse off meat packages and dice jalapeno peppers. Open the meat packages and add peppers to the packages. Place the meat packages in a hot pot to heat for 1 hour. While waiting, crush the chips fairly fine and slice the pickle as you would for a burger. Once hot, pour the meat packages into the chip bag and knead. Flatten the mixture out in
the bag as you would a pizza. Wrap in a towel or newspaper. Allow to cook for 15 minutes. Unwrap burgers and cut open the bag. Using your ID card, cut burgers the size of your bread. You should make 10 burgers. Place 1 burger on a slice of bread and top with cheese, pickle, hot sauce, and salad dressing. If onions are available, add them to the toppings. Only big ballers need to eat this one!

We have to do the best we are capable of.
This is our sacred human responsibility.
– Albert Einstein

Cheeseburger Helper

Ingredients
2 (3 oz.) beef Ramen noodles
1 (8 oz.) package Mexican beef
1 (2 oz.) package ranch dressing
1/4 (16 oz.) bottle squeeze cheese
1/2 (5 oz.) summer sausage
4 slices bread
2 packages beef Ramen seasoning
3 coffee mugs hot water
1 teaspoon onion flakes
2 tablespoons butter

Directions
In a large spread bowl, combine Ramen and hot water. Cook Ramen without seasonings. Cover the bowl tightly and steep for 5 minutes. While waiting, dice summer sausage. Drain any water after cooking and rinse the Ramen in cold water to remove starch. Set bread and butter aside and using a large clean chip bag combine the remaining ingredients and mix well. Double bag and place the bag in a hot pot. Allow this to heat for 2 hours. Stir occasionally. Once cooked, pour the mixture into your spread bowl and butter your bread. This is a delicious meal for one hungry individual.

In every sense, fitness is at the heart of the business of living.
– Malcolm Forbes

Cheese Steak Sandwich

Ingredients
1 (11.25 oz.) package BBQ beef
1/2 (9 oz.) dill pickle
4 slices bread
4 tablespoons squeeze cheese
2 tablespoons onion flakes
1 (3 oz.) jalapeno pepper (single)
2 tablespoons salad dressing
salt and pepper to taste

Directions
Separate the beef pieces from the BBQ sauce and rinse the beef. Set the BBQ sauce aside. In a rice bag, combine beef pieces and onion flakes. Place the bag in a hot pot and heat for 30 minutes. While waiting, dice the pickle and jalapeno pepper. Once the meat is hot, separate it into two equal parts. Add one half to a slice of bread and top with half the pickle, jalapeno peppers, salad dressing, cheese, and salt and pepper. Place another piece of bread on top. Repeat steps for the second sandwich. If you don't want to waste BBQ sauce, whip up some instant potatoes and top with BBQ sauce.

*The human spirit can endure in sickness,
but a crushed spirit, who can bear?
– Proverbs 18:14*

Chip and Cheese Burger

Ingredients
1 (6 oz.) bag Salsa Verde chips
4 tablespoons refried beans
1/4 (9 oz.) dill pickle
1 teaspoon onion flakes
4 tablespoons squeeze cheese
hot sauce to taste
1 (8 oz.) package Mexican beef
8 tablespoons hot water
1 (1.3 oz.) jalapeno pepper (single)
4 slices of bread
2 tablespoons salad dressing

Directions
Crush Salsa Verde chips. Add Mexican beef, refried beans, and hot water to the bag and knead. Separate the mixture into two equal parts and form patties. Place patties in a clean rice bag and heat in a hot pot 2 hours. While heating, cut up the pickle and jalapeno pepper into pieces. Hydrate onion flakes with a few drops of hot water. Once cooked, place one patty on a slice of bread and top with half the pickle, jalapeno pepper, onion flakes, cheese, salad dressing, and hot sauce. Top with another piece of bread. Repeat steps for the second sandwich. Grab a cold drink and a few chips.

You have as much laughter as you have faith.
– Martin Luther

Just Like Home Spaghetti

Ingredients
2 (8 oz.) packages Mexican ground beef
2 teaspoons sweetener or 4 tablespoons sugar
1 teaspoon black pepper
4 slices of bread
1 coffee mug ketchup
2 (3 oz.) beef Ramen noodles
3 coffee mugs hot water
2 tablespoons butter

Directions
In a large, clean chip bag, combine meat packages, ketchup, and sweeteners (or sugar), and mix well. Double bag and place in a hot pot to heat for 2 hours. Use the hottest pot available. Stir occasionally. Just prior to the sauce being ready, in a large spread bowl, lightly crush the Ramen and then add black pepper and hot water. Cover the bowl tightly and steep for 5 minutes. Drain all water. Pour sauce over Ramen and mix well. Butter up your bread and dig in.

I am convinced digestion is the great secret of life.
– Sydney Smith

Troy Traylor

Now That's Spaghetti

Ingredients
1 (5 oz.) summer sausage
1 (11.25 oz.) package chili no beans
2 heaping tablespoons onion flakes
1 coffee mug ketchup
1 heaping teaspoon black pepper
2 (1.3 oz.) jalapeno peppers (single)
1 (12 oz.) V-8 juice
1/2 (12 oz.) can water
1 tablespoon garlic powder
2 (3 oz.) chili Ramen noodles
1/2 (11 oz.) bag cheese puffs

Directions
Dice summer sausage and jalapeno peppers into small pieces. In a large, clean chip bag, combine all the ingredients, except Ramen, black pepper, and cheese puffs, and mix well. Double bag and place in a hot pot to heat for 3 hours. Stir occasionally. In a large spread bowl, just prior to the sauce being ready, lightly crush Ramen and then add black pepper with 3 1/2 coffee mugs of hot water. Cover the bowl tightly and steep for 5 minutes. Drain excess water. Once the sauce is ready, pour it over the top of the Ramen and mix well. Crush cheese puffs and sprinkle over the top. Lightly stir. Best served with buttered bread.

It is a disgrace to grow old through sheer carelessness.
– Socrates

Pot Roast Perfection

Ingredients
1 (1.3 oz.) jalapeno pepper (single)
1/4 (8 oz.) bag instant white rice
1 (12 oz.) V-8 or tomato juice
1 (11.25 oz.) package pot roast
4 tablespoons squeeze cheese
3 1/4 coffee mugs hot water
1 1/2 coffee mugs instant potatoes (any flavor)

Directions
Dice jalapeno pepper. In a clean, large chip bag, combine pepper pieces, rice, V-8 juice, and pot roast. Mix well. Double bag and cook in a hot pot for 45 minutes. Stir occasionally. Now add cheese to the bag and place it back in the hot pot for an additional hour. You may need to add a 1/4 cup of water to this as it cooks, to keep it moist. Just before the roast is done, combine instant potatoes and hot water in a large mixing bowl. Add water slowly as you whip. Adjust as needed. Your potatoes should be on the thick side. Remove mixture from hot pot, pile potatoes in the center of the bowl, and pour pot roast over the top. This one is simply delicious.

The brain is wider than the sky.
– Emily Dickinson

Quick Snack

Ingredients
1 (11.25 oz.) package chili no beans
1 (11.25 oz.) package BBQ beef
2 (1.3 oz.) jalapeno peppers (singles)
1 (16 oz.) bag tortilla chips
1/4 (16 oz.) bottle squeeze cheese
2 coffee mugs refried beans
3 1/2 coffee mugs hot water

Directions
Rinse off meat packages and place in a hot pot to heat for 30 minutes. While waiting, in a large spread bowl, combine refried beans and hot water. Cover bowl tightly and steep for 10 minutes. Dice jalapeno peppers into small pieces. When the meat packages are hot, add jalapeno pieces and both meat packages to the spread bowl and mix well. Now top with cheese. Eat as a dip with your favorite drink. This can also be layered, if you choose. It is a quick, fast, and good meal.

I am not my body. My body is nothing without me.
– Tom Stoppard

Sheppard's Pie

Ingredients
1 (4 oz.) serving corn from tray
1 (8 oz.) package Mexican ground beef
1 (4 oz.) serving green beans from tray
1/2 teaspoon garlic powder
1 teaspoon habanero sauce
3 coffee mugs hot water
1/2 teaspoon onion powder
4 tablespoons squeeze cheese
1 1/2 coffee mugs favorite instant potatoes
salt and pepper to taste

Directions
Using a rice bag, combine all the ingredients except the instant potatoes and hot water. Mix well and cook in a hot pot for 3 hours. Stir occasionally. Once cooked, using a large spread bowl, combine the instant potatoes and hot water and mix until lumps are dissolved. Potatoes should be thick. Best to add water a little at a time. Pour the bag mixture into a bowl and mix well. There you have it: a very good meal. You can add a summer sausage to this if you desire.

I am always busy, which is perhaps the chief reason why I am always well.
– Elizabeth Cady Stanton

Smothered Potatoes

Ingredients
1 (11.25 oz.) package BBQ beef
1 1/2 coffee mugs instant potatoes (any flavor)
1 (1.3 oz.) jalapeno pepper (single)
1/2 teaspoon onion powder
3 coffee mugs hot water

Directions
Dice jalapeno pepper into small pieces. Rinse off the meat package and open it. Add pepper pieces and onion powder to the meat package. Stir the ingredients well and then heat them in a hot pot for 30 minutes. Right before you remove the mixture from the hot pot, combine instant potatoes and one-half of the hot water in a large spread bowl. Mix well. Slowly add more water as you whip. Your goal is to have no lumps or clumps and a stiff consistency. Once the meat package is hot, pour it over the potatoes.

He was going to live forever or die in the attempt.
– Joseph Heller

Sweet Ole' Pot Roast

Ingredients
2 (1.3 oz.) jalapeno peppers (singles)
1 (11.25 oz.) package pot roast
1/2 (8 oz.) bag instant rice (white or brown)
1 (12 oz.) orange juice
a pinch each of salt and black pepper
1 (8 oz.) Mexican ground beef
1 tablespoon habanero sauce
3 tablespoons squeeze cheese

Directions
Dice jalapeno peppers small and remove seeds. Using a large, clean chip bag, combine all the ingredients, except the cheese. Mix well. Double bag and cook in a hot pot for 1 1/2 hours. Stir occasionally. You may need to add a tablespoon or two of water to keep moist. Once cooked, pour the contents into a large spread bowl and mix well. Top with cheese. This is a nice meal with saltine crackers or buttered bread.

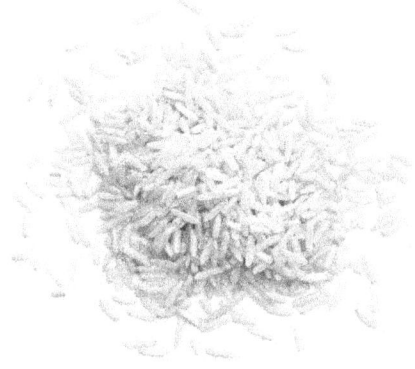

A goal should scare you a little and excite you a lot.
– Joe Vitale

Tangy Summer Sausage & Rice

Ingredients
1 (5 oz.) summer sausage
2 (1.3 oz.) jalapeno peppers (singles)
1/2 (8 oz.) bag instant white rice
1 coffee mug hot water
2 teaspoons lemon-lime electrolyte or 4 tbsps. lemon Kool-Aid
1 sleeve saltine crackers (optional)

Directions
Dice summer sausage and jalapeno peppers into small pieces. Using a clean rice bag, combine the rice and hot water. Wrap the bag in a towel for 12 minutes. Drain any remaining water. Now, put the rice in a large spread bowl and add the summer sausage and jalapeno pepper pieces. Stir well. Now add the electrolyte and stir again until all is coated. Eat as is or with saltine crackers.

As grandmothers used to say,
"Better to pay the grocer than the doctor."
– Michael Pollan

Section 6:
Chicken Dishes

Troy Traylor

Poultry-Facts & History

Wikipedia

Poultry (/'poultri/) are domesticated birds kept by humans for their eggs, their meat, or their feathers. These birds are most typically members of the superorder *Galloanserae* (fowl), especially the order *Galliformes* (which includes chickens, quails, and turkeys).

Poultry also includes other birds that are killed for their meat, such as the young of pigeons (known as squabs), but does not include similar wild birds hunted for sport or food and known as game. The word "poultry" comes from the French/Norman word *poule*, itself derived from the Latin word *pullus*, which means small animal.

The domestication of poultry took place several thousand years ago. This may have originally been a result of people hatching and rearing young birds from eggs collected from the wild, but later involved keeping the birds permanently in captivity. Domesticated chickens may have been used for cockfighting at first and quail kept for their songs, but soon it was realized how useful it was to have a captive-bred source of food.

Selective breeding for fast growth, egg-laying ability, conformation, plumage, and docility took place over the centuries, and modern breeds often look very different from their wild ancestors. Although some birds are still kept in small flocks in extensive systems, most birds available in the market today are reared in intensive commercial enterprises.

Together with pig meat, poultry is one of the two most widely eaten types of meat globally, with over 70% of the meat supply in 2012 between them; poultry provides nutritionally beneficial food containing high-quality protein accompanied by a low proportion of fat. All poultry meat should be properly handled and sufficiently cooked in order to reduce the risk of food poisoning.

The word "poultry" comes from the Middle English *pultrie*, from Old French *pouletrie*, from *pouletier*, poultry dealer, from *poulet*, pullet. The word "pullet" itself comes from Middle English *pulet*, from Old French *polet*, both from Latin *pullus*, a young fowl, young animal, or chicken. The word "fowl" is of a Germanic origin (cf, Old English *fugol*, German *vogel*, Danish *fugl*).

Definition

"Poultry" is a term used for any kind of domesticated bird, captive raised for its utility, and traditionally the word has been used to refer to wildfowl (*galliformes*) and waterfowl (*anseriformes*), but not to cage birds, such as songbirds and parrots. "Poultry" can be defined as domestic fowls, including chickens, turkeys, geese, and ducks, raised for the production of meat or eggs, and the word is also used for the flesh of these birds used as food.

The Encyclopedia Britannica lists the same bird groups but also includes guinea fowl and squabs (young pigeons). In R.D. Crawford's *Poultry Breeding and Genetics*, squabs are Omitted, but Japanese quail and common pheasant are added to the list, the latter frequently being bred in captivity and released into the wild. In his 1848 classic book on poultry, *Ornamental and Domestic Poultry and Management*, Edmund Dixon included chapters on the peafowl, guinea fowl, mute swan, turkey, various types of geese, the Muscovy duck, other ducks, and all types of chickens, including bantams.

In colloquial speech, the term "fowl" is often used near-synonymously with "domesticated chicken" (*gallus gallus*), or with "poultry" or even just "bird," and many languages do not distinguish between "poultry" and "fowl." Both words are also used for the flesh of these birds. Poultry can be distinguished from "game," defined as wild birds or mammals hunted for food or sport, a word also used to describe the flesh of these when eaten.

Poultry as Food

Poultry is the second most widely eaten type of meat in the world, accounting for about 30% of total meat production worldwide compared to pork at 38%. Sixteen billion birds are raised annually for consumption, more than half of these in industrialized, factory-like production units. Global broiler meat production rose to 84.6 million metric tons in 2013. The largest producers were the United States (20%), China (16.6%), Brazil (15.1%), and the European Union (11.3%). There are two distinct models of production; the European Union supply chain model seeks to supply products that can be traced back to the farm of origin. The model faces the increasing cost of implementing additional food safety requirements, welfare issues, and environmental regulations. In contrast, the United States model turns the product into a commodity.

World production of duck meat was about 4.2 million metric tons in 2011, with China producing two-thirds of the total, some 1.7 billion birds. Other notable duck-producing countries in the Far East include Vietnam, Thailand, Malaysia, Myanmar, Indonesia, and South Korea (12% in total). France (3.5%) is the largest producer in the West, followed by other EU nations (3%) and North America (1.7%). China was also by far the largest producer of goose fowl meat, with a 94% share of the 2.6 million metric tons global market.

Cuts of Poultry

Poultry is available fresh or frozen, as whole birds or as joints (cuts), bone-in or deboned, seasoned in various ways, raw or ready cooked. The meatiest parts of a bird are the flight muscles on its chest, called "breast" meat, and the walking muscles on the legs, called the "thigh" and "drumstick." The wings are also eaten (Buffalo wings are a popular example in the United States) and may be split into three segments: the meatier "drumette," the "wingette" (also called the "flat"), and the wing tip (also called the "flapper").

Fine Dining Prison Cookbook 2

BBQ Chicken

Ingredients
1 (7 oz.) package chicken chunks
1 tablespoon onion flakes
1/2 teaspoon garlic powder
2 tablespoons hot sauce of choice
1/4 (18 oz.) bottle BBQ sauce (1/3 coffee mug)

Directions
Rinse off the meat package and open it. Add all the ingredients to the package. Heat the package in a hot pot for 3 hours. Remove and serve. Great meal with instant potatoes and sweet and sour rice.

*Magic is believing in yourself;
if you can do that, you can make anything happen.
– Johann Wolfgang von Goethe*

Troy Traylor

Cheesy Chicken Burritos

Ingredients
1 (7 oz.) package chicken chunks
1/2 (8 oz.) bag instant white rice
2 1/2 coffee mugs hot water
1 (8 oz.) bag jalapeno chips
1/4 (16 oz.) bottle squeeze cheese
1 package chicken Ramen seasoning
6 flour tortillas

Directions
Drain and shred chicken chunks. In a large spread bowl, combine rice and hot water. Cover bowl tightly and steep for 10 minutes. Crush jalapeno chips while you wait. Once rice is cooked, drain any remaining water. To the chip bag, add the chicken chunks, rice, squeeze cheese, Ramen seasoning, and a 1/4 coffee mug of hot water. Lightly knead, double bag, and place the bag in a hot pot to cook for 1 hour. Remove from the hot pot and spoon the mixture onto flour tortillas. You can enjoy this as is, but I like to place 4 in a rice bag and cook in a hot pot for 2-3 hours. Add any toppings you desire. This is also great with some party mix and a cold drink.

It is easier to change a man's religion than to change his diet.
– Margaret Mead

Chicken-Chili Nachos

Ingredients
2 (11.25 oz.) packages chicken chili
2 (1.3 oz.) jalapeno peppers (singles)
1 (16 oz.) bag tortilla chips
1 (6 oz.) bag Salsa Verde chips
1 coffee mug refried beans
1 1/4 coffee mugs hot water
1/4 bottle squeeze cheese

Directions
Rinse off meat packages and heat in a hot pot for 30 minutes. Use the highest-temperature pot available. While waiting, dice the jalapeno peppers into small pieces. Crush Salsa Verde chips into a fine powder. Using a large spread bowl, combine the refried beans and hot water. Cover the bowl tightly and steep for 10 minutes. Once the meat in packages is hot, pour into refried beans and add Salsa Verde chips and squeeze cheese. Stir well. Layer a separate bowl with tortilla chips and half of the bean mixture. Repeat steps once again. Can also use it as a dip if you would like. To spice it up, add hot sauce on top.

I enjoy perfect health, which I wish I could ruin again, but age prevents me.
– Giacomo Casanova

Troy Traylor

Chicken & Dumplings

Ingredients
1 (7 oz.) package chicken chunks
1 (3 oz.) chicken Ramen noodles (crushed)
1 (4 oz.) serving green beans from tray
1 (4 oz.) serving carrots from tray
1 teaspoon black pepper
2 packages chicken Ramen seasoning
1 teaspoon onion powder
1 tablespoon onion flakes
1 teaspoon garlic powder
3 tablespoons corn starch (optional)
1 heaping shot squeeze cheese
2 coffee mugs hot water
6 flour tortillas
1/2 coffee mug instant milk

Directions
Using a large chip bag, combine all the ingredients except the flour tortillas. Mix until the starch is dissolved. Double bag and cook in a hot pot for 3 1/2 hours. Stir occasionally. Add water if needed to keep a little wet. Once cooked, tear tortillas into quarters and roll up into balls. Add them to the bag and cook for another hour. Your mixture should be smooth and creamy.

Let life go on in [your body] unhindered and let it defend itself; it will be more effective than if you paralyze it by encumbering it with remedies.
– Leo Tolstoy

Chicken Salad

Ingredients
1 tablespoon onion flakes
1 heaping tablespoon relish
1 (7 oz.) package chicken chunks
1 package chicken Ramen seasoning
1/4 (9 oz.) dill pickle
1/2 teaspoon black pepper
2 tablespoons salad dressing
3 hard-boiled eggs

Directions
Hydrate the onion flakes with a few drops of hot water. Dice the pickle. In a spread bowl, combine all ingredients except the eggs and mix well. Dice the eggs and fold them into the mixture. Serve on bread, crackers, or tortilla chips.

He is the best physician that knows the worthlessness of most medicines.
– Benjamin Franklin

Troy Traylor

Chicken Spaghetti

Ingredients
1 (12 oz.) V-8 juice
1 (7 oz.) package chicken chunks
2 (3 oz.) chicken Ramen noodles
2 packages chicken Ramen seasoning
1 light teaspoon garlic powder
2 tablespoons salsa or picante sauce
1 coffee mug of ketchup

Directions
Set Ramen aside. Combine all remaining ingredients in a large chip bag. Double the bag, and heat in a hot pot for 3 hours. After 2 hours and 15 minutes, remove the Ramen from its package and add it to the bag. Stir well. Do not break the noodles. Place the bag back into the hot pot to cook for the remaining 45 minutes. Fill up your bowl and dig in just like Momma used to make!

*The world is full of magic things,
patiently waiting for our senses to grow sharper.
– W.B. Yeats*

Fine Dining Prison Cookbook 2

Easy Baked Chicken

Ingredients
1 sleeve Matzo crackers or Golden Round crackers
1 (5.6 oz.) package Marias Cookies
2 (7 oz.) packages chicken chunks
1 heaping tablespoon instant milk
3 tablespoons ketchup
2 tablespoons mustard
1 package chili seasoning from Ramen
3 tablespoons hot water

Directions
Crush crackers and Marias cookies into a fine powder. In a large spread bowl, combine all the ingredients and mix well. Divide the mixture and form each into a drumstick. Place these in a large chip bag, double bag, and cook in a hot pot for 1 hour. Serve in your spread bowl and eat up. You can glaze these with BBQ sauce if you desire.

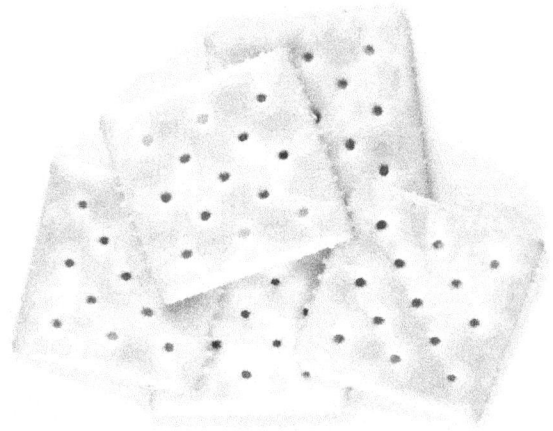

It is not in the stars to hold our destiny but in ourselves.
– William Shakespeare

Lemon-Pepper Chicken

Ingredients
1 (12 oz.) Sprite
1 (7 oz.) package chicken chunks
1/2 (8 oz.) bag instant white rice
12 pieces of lemon candy
1 teaspoon lemon lime electrolyte or 4 tbsp. lemon Kool-Aid
3 tablespoons salad dressing
1/2 teaspoon black pepper
1/2 can hot water

Directions
Crush candies and place in an insert cup with hot water and electrolytes. Set in a hot pot and stir until the candies dissolve. Use the hottest pot available. Once dissolved, in a large chip bag, combine all ingredients, double bag, and heat in a hot pot for 2 hours. You may need to add shots of water as this cooks. Stir occasionally. These sure beat anything in the chow hall.

Health nuts are going to feel stupid someday, lying in hospital beds dying of nothing.
– Redd Foxx

Fine Dining Prison Cookbook 2

Orange Chicken with Sweet & Spicy Glaze

Ingredients
2 (1.3 oz.) jalapeno peppers (singles)
1 (12 oz.) pineapple orange juice
1 (7 oz.) package chicken chunks
1 (3 oz.) chicken Ramen noodles
1 (3 oz.) chili Ramen noodles
1 (2 oz.) package hot peanuts
1 fireball candy (crushed)
1 teaspoon habanero sauce
1 package chicken Ramen seasoning
2 teaspoons sweetener or 4 tablespoons of sugar
2 tablespoons salad dressing
2 coffee mugs hot water
5 tablespoons squeeze cheese

Directions
Dice jalapeno pepper. Combine 6 tablespoons of pineapple orange juice, one sweetener, pepper pieces, and the crushed fireball in an insert cup. Stir and set aside while preparing the rest. Open the chicken chunks package and add 1 package of sweetener and  enough juice to cover the chicken chunks. Marinate for 2 hours and then place the package in a hot pot for 1 hour. Just prior to pulling out the meat package, add salad dressing and habanero sauce to the insert cup and stir well. Now add cheese to insert and whip until creamy. Remove the meat package from the hot

pot and set the insert cup in the hot pot for 15 minutes. Stir occasionally. Use the hottest pot available. Using a large chip bag, combine both Ramen noodles, the remaining juice, and hot water. Add 1/2 of the chili seasoning to this. Knead, then tie the bag and wrap it in a towel. Cook for 8 minutes. Once all is ready, drain any remaining juices from the Ramen and place all in a large spread bowl. Pour the meat package contents over the Ramen and mix well. Sprinkle chicken seasoning package over top and top off with peanuts. Stir well. Remove the insert cup from the hot pot and pour evenly over the top of the dish. Lightly mix. This is one amazing meal!

We did not come to fear the future.
We came here to shape it.
– Barack Obama

Sweet Chicken & Rice

Ingredients
1 chicken quarter from tray
1 (12 oz.) orange juice
1 package chicken Ramen seasoning
2 teaspoons sweetener or 4 tablespoons sugar
1/4 (8 oz.) bag instant white rice
1 (2 oz.) package salted peanuts

Directions
Shred chicken quarters. Set the peanuts aside. Using a large chip bag, combine all remaining ingredients and mix well. Double bag and place in a hot pot to heat for 2 hours. Once the cook time is complete, drain the juices and place the mixture in a spread bowl. Add the peanuts and stir well. Nice change from the mundane foods from the chow hall.

*Don't judge each day by the harvest you reap
but by the seeds that you plant.
– Robert Louis Stevenson*

Sweet & Sour Chicken & Rice

Ingredients
1 (1.3 oz.) jalapeno pepper (single)
1 (12 oz.) pineapple orange juice
2 tablespoons of sweetener or 4 tablespoons of sugar
2 tablespoons pickle juice
1 (7 oz.) package chicken chunks
1/2 (8 oz.) bag instant white rice
1/2 coffee mug hot water

Directions
Dice jalapeno pepper. In a large clean chip bag, combine all the ingredients. Mix well and double bag. Cook in a hot pot for 2 hours. Stir occasionally and add water as needed to keep moist. If no pineapple orange juice is available, use regular orange juice. "MMM Good!"

Sometimes you have to get sicker before you can get better.
– Jeannette Walls

Tahitian Chicken

Ingredients
1 (7 oz.) package chicken chunks or 2 chicken quarters
1/4 coffee mug butter
1/3 onion or 2 tablespoons onion flakes
2 tablespoons soy sauce
1 (12 oz.) pineapple orange juice
1/4 coffee mug brown sugar
1 (4 oz.) serving pineapple chunks from tray
2 tablespoons cornstarch
6 tablespoons hot water
1 (2 oz.) package energy mix

Directions
Shred chicken and dice onion. If soy sauce is not available, see the recipe in this book to make your own. Using a large chip bag, combine all ingredients, except the energy mix, and mix well. Double bag and tie up. Allow this to marinate for 2 hours, and then place the bag in a hot pot to cook for an additional 3 hours. Stir occasionally. Once cooked, drain all juices into a small bowl or cup. Place the mixture in a large spread bowl and top with the energy mix. Lightly mix. A side of potatoes is nice with this meal. Use juices to mix in potatoes. As you can see, you will need a little help from the kitchen for this meal.

I take the true definition of exercise to be, labor without weariness.
– Samuel Johnson 1709-1784

Helpful Cooking Tips

Create your own colored sugar by placing granulated sugar in a plastic bag. Add a few drops of your favorite food coloring and shake to blend. Pour out onto a plate and let dry, then use.

Try using raw spaghetti instead of toothpicks when securing stuffed chicken breasts and meats. It works great and it's edible!

When baking and you need to "cut in" the butter, an easy way is to keep the sticks of butter in the freezer. When needed, use a cheese grater to grate the butter into fine pieces.

To get snowy white potatoes, add a teaspoon of vinegar or fresh lemon juice to the boiling water.

When making potato salad, add the dressing to warm potatoes for the best flavor. Once cooled, the potatoes will not absorb the dressing as well.

Slide a strand of unwaxed dental floss – one end wrapped around the forefingers of each hand – under fresh cookies to unstick them from a cookie sheet. Floss also makes a clean cut through a cake for layering. No more crumbly edges!

For extra smooth, well-mixed oil and vinegar salad dressing: Combine all ingredients in a screw top jar, add an ice cube and shake then discard what's left of the ice cube.

If you put onions in the freezer 15 minutes before you chop them, you'll reduce the spray of vaporized onion oils, which means your eyes won't tear when you cut the onions.

To prevent cream whipped ahead of time from separating, add one-quarter teaspoon of gelatin to each cup of cream during whipping.

A jar lid or a couple of marbles in the bottom half of a double boiler will rattle when the water gets low and warn you to add more before the pan scorches or burns.

Section 7:
Fish Dishes

Troy Traylor

Seafood Facts & History

Wikipedia

The harvesting and consumption of seafood are ancient practices that may date back to at least the Upper Paleolithic period, which dates back to between 50,000 and 10,000 years ago. Isotopic analysis of the skeletal remains of Tianyuan man, a 40,000-year-old modern human from eastern Asia, has shown that he regularly consumed freshwater fish. Archaeology features such as shell middens, discarded fish bones, and cave paintings show that seafoods were important for survival and consumed in significant quantities. During this period, most people lived a hunter-gatherer lifestyle and were, of necessity, constantly on the move. However, where there are early examples of permanent settlements (though not necessarily permanently occupied), such as those at Lepenski Vir, they are almost always associated with fishing as a major source of food.

The ancient River Nile was full of fish; fresh and dried fish were a staple food for much of the population. The Egyptians had implements and methods for fishing, and these are illustrated in tomb scenes, drawings, and papyrus documents. Some representations hint at fishing being pursued as a pastime.

Ancient Israelites

The Israelites ate a variety of fresh and saltwater fish, according to both archaeological and textual evidence. Remains of freshwater fish from the Yarkon and Jordan rivers and the Sea of Galilee have been found in excavations and include St. Peter's fish and mouthbreeders. Saltwater fish discovered in excavations include sea bream, grouper, meager, and gray mullet. Most of these come from the Mediterranean, but in the later Iron Age period, some are from the Red Sea. Fishermen supplied fish to inland communities, as remains of fish, including bones and scales, have been discovered at many inland sites.

To preserve them for transport, the fish were first smoked or dried and salted. Merchants also imported fish, sometimes from as far as Egypt, where pickled roe was an export article. Remains of Nile Perch from Egypt have been found, and these must have been smoked or dried before being imported through the trade network that connected ancient Near Eastern societies.

Merchants shipped fish to Jerusalem, and there was evidently a significant trade in fish; one of the gates of Jerusalem was called the Fish Gate, named for a fish market nearby. Fish products were salted and dried and sent great distances during the Israelite and Judean monarchies. However, even in later Persian, Greek, and Roman periods, the cost of preserving and transporting fish must have meant that only wealthier inhabitants of the highland towns and cities could afford it, or those who lived close to the sources, where it was less expensive.

Ancient Greece

Fishing scenes are rarely represented in ancient Greek culture, a reflection of the low social status of fishing. The consumption of fish varied in accordance with the wealth and location of the household. In the Greek islands and on the coast, fresh fish and Seafood (squid, octopus, and shellfish) was common. They were eaten locally, but more often transported inland. Sardines and anchovies were sometimes sold fresh, but more frequently salted. A stele of the late 3rd century BCE from the small Boeotian city of Akraiphia, on Lake Copais, provides us with a list of fish prices. The cheapest was skaren (probably parrotfish), whereas Atlantic bluefin tuna was three times as expensive. Common saltwater fish were yellowfin tuna, red mullet, ray, swordfish, or sturgeon, a delicacy which was eaten salted. Lake Copais itself was famous in all Greece for its eels, celebrated by the hero of The Acharnians. Other freshwater fish were pike, carp, and the less appreciated catfish.

Ancient Rome

Pictorial evidence of Roman fishing comes from mosaics. The Greco-Roman sea god Neptune is depicted as wielding a fishing trident. Fish was served only in earlier periods, and it remained more expensive than simpler meat types. Breeding was attempted in freshwater and saltwater ponds, but some kinds of fish could not be fattened in captivity. Among these was the formidable and potentially toxic Mediterranean moray, a valued delicacy that was reared in ponds at the seaside. These morays were also kept as pets and sometimes as a means of punishment. Another farmed species was the popular mullus, the goatfish. At a certain time, this fish was considered the epitome of luxury, above all because its scales exhibit a bright red color when it dies out of water. For this reason, these fish were occasionally allowed to die slowly at the table. There was even a recipe where this would take place in garo, in the sauce.

At the beginning of the Imperial era, however, this custom suddenly came to an end, which is why mullus in the feast of Trimalchio (see the Satyricon) could be shown as a characteristic of the parvenu, who bores a guest with an unfashionable display of dying fish. The fish and fishing practices of the Roman era were recorded by the Greco-Roman Oppian of Cilicia, whose *Halieutics* was an expansive poem in hexameter composed between 177 and 180. It is the earliest such work to have survived to the modern day.

Garum, also known as liquamen, was the universal sauce added to everything. It was prepared by subjecting salted fish, in particular mackerel intestines, to a very slow thermal process. Over the course of two to three months, in an enzymatic process stimulated by heating, usually by exposure to the sun, the protein-laden fish parts are filtered, and the liquid is traded as garum, the remaining solids as alec – a kind of savory spread. Because of the smell it produced, the production of garum within the city was banned. Garum, supplied in small, sealed amphorae, was used throughout the Empire and totally replaced salt as a condiment. Today, similar sauces are produced in Southeast Asia, usually sold abroad under the description "fish sauce" or *nam pla*.

BBQ Mackerel

Ingredients
1/4 (8 oz.) bag instant white rice
1 coffee mug hot water
1/2 (9 oz.) dill pickle
1 coffee mug jalapeno chips (crushed)
2 tablespoons onion flakes
1 heaping tablespoon salad dressing
1/2 (18 oz.) bottle BBQ sauce
1 teaspoon mustard
2 (3.5 oz.) packages mackerel
1/4 (16 oz.) bottle squeeze cheese
2 tablespoons pickle juice
5 tablespoons refried beans
1 (10 oz.) package flour tortillas

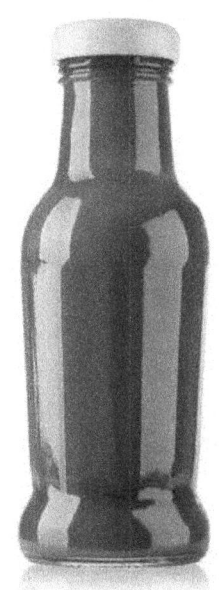

Directions
Combine rice and hot water in a large spread bowl. Cover tightly and steep for 10 minutes. While waiting, dice pickle, crush chips, and drain mackerel. Set flour tortillas aside and combine remaining ingredients in rice bowl and mix. Spoon the mixture onto the flour tortillas and roll. Place 4-5 burritos into a rice bag. Place the bag into a hot pot to cook for 1 hour. You can use a chip bag for cooking but double the bag if you do. Once cooked, place all the ingredients in a spread bowl. You can coat this with extra cheese if you like. It's really good!

Those who worship health cannot remain healthy.
– G.K. Chesterton

Cellblock Cuisine

Ingredients
2 (3 oz.) chili Ramen noodles
3 coffee mugs hot water
1 (3.5 oz.) package mackerel or 1 (4.23 oz.) tuna
1 (9 oz.) dill pickle
1 (4 oz.) serving mixed fruit from tray
1 teaspoon lemon lime electrolyte or 4 tablespoons Kool-Aid
1/4 coffee mug sunflower seeds

Directions
Using a large spread bowl, combine Ramen, seasoning, and hot water. Cover the bowl tightly and steep for 5 minutes. While waiting, drain the mackerel or tuna. Dice the pickle into small pieces. Drain any remaining water from the Ramen. Using a clean, large chip bag, combine Ramen, mackerel, and pickle: double bag and place in a hot pot to cook for 45 minutes. Once cooked, pour the mixture into a large spread bowl and add the remaining ingredients. Mix all thoroughly. Eat while hot.

*If you are not willing to risk the unusual,
you will have to settle for the ordinary.
– Jim Rohn*

Fish Balls

Ingredients
2 (4.23 oz.) packages tuna or 2 (3.5 oz.) packages of mackerel
1/4 (8 oz.) bag jalapeno chips
1 teaspoon coffee
1/4 (8 oz.) bag BBQ chips
1/4 (8 oz.) bag Shabang chips
1 (2 oz.) package cream cheese
3 tablespoons BBQ sauce
1 (2 oz.) package ranch dressing

Directions
Drain and fluff tuna (or mackerel). Crush Shabang and jalapeno chips. Set BBQ chips and ranch dressing aside, and in a large spread bowl, combine the remaining ingredients and knead well. Divide the mixture into several equal parts and roll each into balls. Now, crush the BBQ chips and roll the balls in these chips to coat. Place all in your spread bowl and cover with ranch dressing.

Health is the vital principal of bliss; and exercise, of health.
– James Thomson, 1700-1748, Scottish poet

Fish Boats

Ingredients
4 (9 oz.) dill pickles
1/2 sleeve Golden Round crackers
1 teaspoon onion powder
2 (3.5 oz.) packages mackerel or 2 (4.23 oz.) packages of tuna
1 teaspoon mustard
1 1/2 tablespoons sandwich spread
pinch black pepper
pinch garlic powder

Directions
Slice pickles in half lengthwise and remove seeds to create a hollow space. Set pickles aside and combine the remaining ingredients in a spread bowl and mix well. Now fill the pickles with this mixture. Makes 8 great fish boats.

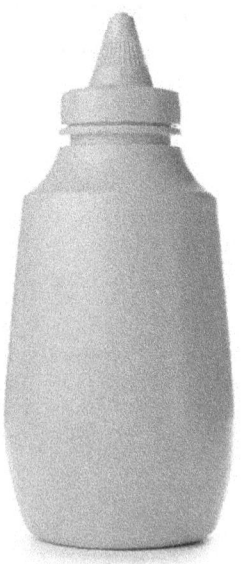

Learn to say "no" to the good so you can say "yes" to the best.
– John C. Maxwell

Fish Creole

Ingredients
1 (4.23 oz.) package tuna
1/4 package chili Ramen seasoning
1 teaspoon onion powder
1/3 coffee mug hot water
1 (3.5 oz.) package mackerel
1/4 package shrimp Ramen seasoning
2 tablespoons salsa
1 (4 oz.) heaping serving okra (from tray)
1 (4 oz.) serving green beans (from tray)
saltine crackers or tortilla chips (optional)

Directions
Drain juices from tuna and mackerel. Using a large chip bag, combine all these ingredients and mix well. Double bag and heat in a hot pot for 2 hours. Once cooked, pour all into a large spread bowl. Enjoy this meal with saltine crackers or tortilla chips.

Recreation is not being idle;
it is easing the wearied part by change of occupation.
– C. Simmons

Troy Traylor

Fish Salad

Ingredients
1 pasta kit **
1 coffee mug hot water
2 (3.5 oz.) packages mackerel or 2 (3.53 oz.) packages sardines
8 pasta shells
1 (2 oz.) package salted peanuts

Directions
Using a large spread bowl, combine the pasta and 1 Italian dressing with the hot water. Cover and steep 6-8 minutes. Drain excess water. Drain the fish and add all remaining ingredients to the bowl and mix well. Might need a little help from an associate with this one.

**A pasta kit comes as a package. It contains some kind of pasta noodles, two Italian dressing packages, and a package of Parmesan cheese.

If you want to go fast, go alone. If you want to go far, go together.
– African proverb

Fish Sticks

Ingredients
1 (3.5 oz.) package mackerel
1/4 (2 oz.) package ranch dressing
1/4 (16 oz.) bag corn chips
1 (4.23 oz.) package tuna
1 coffee mug jalapeno chips (crushed)
1/3 coffee mug hot water

Directions
Drain the mackerel and tuna packages. Using a small bowl, combine mackerel, tuna, and ranch dressing. Mix well. Crush jalapeno chips and add to the mixture. Mix well and set aside. Crush the corn chips into a fine powder. Carefully add enough hot water and knead until all sticks together and is only slightly moist. Place this mixture in a chip bag and flatten evenly. Cut the bag open and, using your ID card, cut dough into 6" x 8" squares. Spoon the fish mixture onto these squares and roll. Place these sticks into a rice bag and cook in a hot pot for 3 hours. After cooking, place in a serving bowl and top with tartar sauce (see recipe in this book), or use a sandwich spread. You have got to love these!

Light is the task where many share the toil.
– Homer

Troy Traylor

Jack Mack Fiesta

Ingredients
1 (3 oz.) chicken Ramen noodles
1/2 (8 oz.) bag instant white rice
3 coffee mugs hot water
1/2 (9 oz.) pickle (any flavor)
2 (1.3 oz.) jalapeno peppers (singles)
1/2 (2.75 oz.) bag pork skins
1 (5 oz.) summer sausage
3 (3.5 oz.) packages mackerel
2 packages chicken Ramen seasoning
1 (2 oz.) package ranch dressing
1 (2 oz.) pack hot peanuts
1/4 (16 oz.) bottle squeeze cheese

Directions
This will be a cold dish. In a large spread bowl, combine the Ramen, rice, and hot water – do not add seasonings. Cover the bowl tightly and steep for 10 minutes. After 10 minutes, drain the water and set aside to cool. While waiting, dice the pickle and jalapeno peppers into small pieces. Crush pork skins lightly and dice summer sausage. Drain the mackerels and combine all ingredients in the spread bowl and mix well. If this is too fishy for you, just add a couple of tablespoons of pickle juice. So good!

Great things never come from comfort zones.
– Neil Strauss

Mackerel Casserole

Ingredients
2 (3 oz.) chicken Ramen noodles
3 (1.3 oz.) jalapeno peppers (singles)
2 (3.5 oz.) packages mackerel
1/4 (16 oz.) bag corn chips
1/4 (16 oz.) bottle squeeze cheese
1 (9 oz.) dill pickle
2 coffee mugs hot water
3 tablespoons salad dressing
1/4 (8 oz.) bag jalapeno chips
2 (2 oz.) packages ranch dressing

Directions
You will need 3 large spread bowls: Lightly crush Ramen and dice pickle and jalapeno peppers. Combine Ramen, seasoning packages, and hot water in a large spread bowl, stir and cover tightly for 10 minutes. While waiting, drain the mackerel. In a second spread bowl, combine mackerel, pickle, pepper pieces, and salad dressing. Mix well. Drain noodles, add them to this bowl, and stir again. In bowl three, layer your ingredients like this: one layer of Ramen mixture, one layer of corn chips, one layer of jalapeno chips, 1/2 the squeeze cheese, and 1 ranch dressing. Repeat these steps one more time. Hope you're really hungry.

A team is a group of people who may not be equal in experience, talent or education but in commitment.
– Patricia Fripp

Mackerel Salad

Ingredients
1 (3.5 oz.) package mackerel
2 hard-boiled eggs
1 (1.3 oz.) jalapeno pepper (single)
1 tablespoon relish
1 teaspoon black pepper
1 tablespoon onion flakes
2 tablespoons squeeze cheese
2 tablespoons salad dressing

Directions
Drain the mackerel package. Cut hard-boiled eggs and jalapeno pepper into small pieces. Using a large spread bowl, combine all the ingredients and stir until well blended. This is best when served on saltine crackers.

The principle of competing is against yourself. It's about self-improvement, about being better than you were the day before.
– Steve Young

Salmon Dogs

Ingredients
1 sleeve Golden Round crackers
1 (2 oz.) package cream cheese
1/2 teaspoon garlic powder
1 (5.6 oz.) package pink salmon
1/4 (9 oz.) dill pickle
1 teaspoon salad dressing
1 teaspoon onion powder
4 flour tortillas

Directions
Crush crackers into a fine powder and dice the pickle. Set flour tortillas aside and combine remaining ingredients in a large spread bowl and mix thoroughly. Cover and allow to sit for 1 hour. Now divide the mixture into 4 equal parts and roll into a hot dog shape. Place one dog on each flour tortilla and roll. Place all 4 in a rice bag and cook in a hot pot for 1 1/2 hours. Once cooked, place all 4 in a spread bowl. You can cover these with cheese, but you really do not need to. Eat with your favorite chips and drink.

*I have the choice of being constantly active and happy
or introspectively passive and sad.
Or I can go mad by ricocheting in between.
– Sylvia Plath*

Troy Traylor

Salmon Salad

Ingredients
1 (5.6 oz.) package pink salmon
1 (1.3 oz.) jalapeno pepper (single)
1 teaspoon onion powder
1 pinch black pepper
1 sleeve Saltine crackers
3 hard-boiled eggs
1/4 (9 oz.) dill pickle
1/2 teaspoon garlic powder
2 heaping tablespoons salad dressing

Directions
Drain the salmon and dice the eggs, jalapeno pepper, and pickle. Set crackers aside and combine remaining ingredients in a large spread bowl. Mix well. Eat on the saltines and wash down with your favorite drink.

Whatever your talents, use them to their fullest.
– Beatrice Warde's headstone, Surrey, England

Savory Paella

Ingredients
4 (3 oz.) chili Ramen noodles
2 coffee mugs hot water
2 tablespoons chili garlic sauce
1 tablespoon peanut butter
1/2 tsp. lemon lime electrolyte or 1 heaping tbsp. lemon Kool-Aid
1/2 teaspoon coffee
2 (2 oz.) packages salted peanuts
1 (3.5 oz.) package mackerel in siracha
1 (3.53 oz.) package tuna with jalapeno peppers

Directions
Lightly crush the Ramen. Set peanuts and both fish packages aside, and using a large chip bag, combine all the remaining ingredients. Mix well. Double bag and wrap in a towel for 10 minutes. Once cooked, equally divide the mixture between 2 bowls and equally divide the remaining ingredients in these bowls. Mix well. Better invite an associate unless you're really hungry.

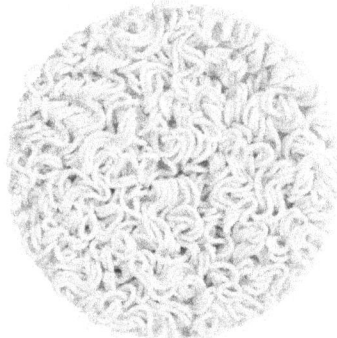

*Success is a state of mind.
If you want success start thinking of yourself as a success.
– Dr. Joyce Brothers*

Super-Seas Delight

Ingredients
1/2 (9 oz.) pickle
1 (3.5 oz.) package mackerel
1 (4.23 oz.) package tuna
2 (2 oz.) packages trail mix
3 (1.3 oz.) jalapeno peppers (singles)
1 (3.53 oz.) package sardines
1 (10 oz.) package flour tortillas
1/2 coffee mug salsa
3 tablespoons salad dressing
1/4 coffee mug squeeze cheese
2 tablespoons hot sauce of choice
2 tablespoons pickle juice

Directions
You will need 2 hot pots. Dice the pickle and jalapeno peppers into small pieces. Drain all juices from meat packages. Using a large spread bowl, combine all ingredients, except the flour tortillas. Mix thoroughly. Now, spoon the mixture onto the tortillas and roll up. In a rice bag, place 4-5 burritos in each bag. Cook in a hot pot for 45 minutes. Repeat until ingredients are exhausted. You can use chip bags to cook in, but if so, double bag. A stiff side of refried beans goes well with this meal.

*If you want something you never had,
you have to do something you've never done.
– Thomas Jefferson*

Sweet & Sour Mackerel

Ingredients
1 (1.3 oz.) jalapeno pepper (single)
1 (3.5 oz.) package mackerel
2 teaspoons of sweetener or 4 tablespoons of sugar
1/2 (8 oz.) bag instant white rice
2 teaspoons pickle juice
2 (12 oz.) pineapple orange juice

Directions
Dice jalapeno pepper and drain juices from mackerel. Using a large, clean chip bag, combine all ingredients and mix well. Double bag and tie up. Heat this bag in a hot pot for 2 hours. Stir occasionally. Once cooked, drain any juices and pour the mixture into a large spread bowl. This dish is simply delicious.

When you soar like an eagle you attract hunters.
– Milton S. Gould

Tahitian Mackerel

Ingredients
1 (3.5 oz.) package mackerel
1 (2 oz.) package energy mix
1 (4 oz.) serving fruit cocktail or pineapples from tray
1 (12 oz.) orange juice
1 1/2 tablespoons corn starch
1 tsp. lemon lime electrolyte or 4 tbsps. Kool Aid
1 1/2 tablespoons mustard
1/3 onion (or 3 tablespoons onion flakes)
1/4 coffee mug melted butter
1/4 coffee mug brown sugar
2 tablespoons soy sauce

Directions
As you can see from these ingredients, you will need a little help from the kitchen. For soy sauce, use the recipe in this book if it is not available at the unit. Now, set aside the energy mix. Dice onion, if available. Using a large clean chip bag, combine all the ingredients, mix well, and double bag. Tie these bags off. Allow this mixture to marinate for 2-3 hours, and then heat it in a hot pot for an additional 2 hours. Once cooked, drain all juices into a cup or small bowl. Pour the mixture into a large spread bowl. Top with the energy mix. This is great with a side of instant rice. If you eat rice with this meal, use juices when preparing this amazing meal!

If at first you don't succeed, try, try again. Then quit. There's no use being a damn fool about it.
– W.C. Fields

Tahitian Tuna

Ingredients
1 (4.23 oz.) package tuna
1 (12 oz.) strawberry kiwi or any fruit juice
1 (2 oz.) package energy mix
1 (4 oz.) serving fruit cocktail from tray
1/3 onion (sub 2 heaping tablespoons onion flakes)
1/4 coffee mug melted butter
1 1/2 tablespoons mustard
1 teaspoon coriander and annatto
2 tablespoons soy sauce
1 tablespoon garlic powder

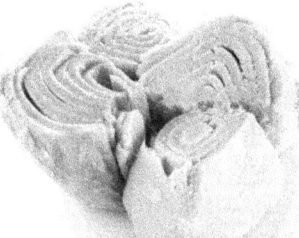

Directions
Dice the onion if available and prepare soy sauce (see recipe if not available at the unit). Set the energy mix aside (can substitute with salted peanuts). Using a large chip bag, combine all ingredients together and mix well. Double bag and tie up. Set the bag aside and let it marinate for 3 hours. Once marinated, heat this bag in a hot pot for 2-3 hours, and then drain the juices from the mixture into a cup or bowl. Place the mixture in your spread bowl and add the energy mix. Mix well. Leftover juices can be used to prepare instant rice. If you are preparing rice, save a little energy mix to put on top.

When you have confidence, you can have a lot of fun. And when you have fun, you can do amazing things.
– Joe Namath

Troy Traylor

Thai Style Fish & Noodles

Ingredients
1 (2 oz.) package trail mix
2 (3 oz.) spicy vegetable Ramen noodles
1 (3.53 oz.) package tuna with jalapeno peppers
1/2 tablespoon garlic powder
3 tablespoons habanero sauce
1 tablespoon peanut butter
2 1/2 coffee mugs hot water

Directions
Remove banana chips from the trail mix and lightly crush Ramen. Using a large chip bag, combine all ingredients and stir until the peanut butter dissolves. Double bag and wrap in a towel for 10 minutes. Once cooked, put all in your spread bowl and dig in.

Success is a series of glorious defeats.
– Mahatma Ghandi

Tuna Salad

Ingredients
few drops hot water
1/4 (9 oz.) dill pickle
1 teaspoon black pepper
2 tablespoons salad dressing
1 light teaspoon garlic powder
1 heaping tablespoon onion flakes
3 hard-boiled eggs
1 (4.23 oz.) package tuna
1 heaping tablespoon relish
1/2 pack chicken Ramen seasoning
4 tablespoons pickle juice

Directions
Hydrate onion flakes in a few drops of hot water. Dice hard-boiled eggs and pickle into small pieces. Using a large spread bowl, combine all ingredients and mix well. You can eat this on bread, crackers, or tortilla chips. Wash all down with your favorite drink. You can drain the tuna if you like, but I prefer not to drain the fish for a stronger taste.

Success is the sum of small efforts, repeated day in and day out.
– Robert Collier

Troy Traylor

Tuna Wraps

Ingredients
1 (2 oz.) package ranch dressing
2 (1.3 oz.) jalapeno peppers (singles)
1 (4.23 oz.) package tuna
2 (2 oz.) packages cream cheese
1 (10 oz.) package flour tortillas
1/4 (16 oz.) bottle squeeze cheese
1/4 (9 oz.) pickle
1/4 (12 oz.) bottle salsa
4 tablespoons refried beans
2 tablespoons onion flakes
1/8 coffee mug hot water
1/2 package shrimp Ramen seasoning

Directions
Dice the pickle and jalapeno peppers into small pieces. In a large spread bowl, combine refried beans, onion flakes, hot water, Ramen seasoning, and pickle pieces. Cover the bowl tightly and steep for 5 minutes. After 5 minutes, drain the tuna, add it to the bowl, and mix well. Mix cream cheese and salsa in a small spread bowl or coffee mug. Whip well. Add this to the tuna mixture and stir well. Separate tortillas and cover with squeeze cheese. Spoon mixture onto tortillas and roll into your wraps. Place 4 wraps in a rice bag and heat in a hot pot for 2 1/2 hours. Once cooked, place 4 wraps in a spread bowl, cover with ranch dressing, and sprinkle your jalapeno pieces over top. This is a great meal to share.

There is nothing noble in being superior to your fellow man; true nobility is being superior to your former self.
– Ernest Hemingway

Fine Dining Prison Cookbook 2

Zee Mack Patty #1

Ingredients
1 (3.5 oz.) package mackerel
2 (1.3 oz.) jalapeno peppers (singles)
1 (2 oz.) package ranch dressing
1/2 (9 oz.) dill pickle
4 cheese and chive crackers from 1 (1.375 oz.) package
4 slices bread
squeeze cheese and salad dressing to taste

Directions
Drain most of the juice from the mackerel. Crush crackers and dice jalapeno peppers. In a large spread bowl, combine mackerel, crackers, jalapeno peppers, and ranch dressing. Mix well and divide into 2 equal parts. Form patties out of this.
Place both patties in a clean rice bag and heat in a hot pot for 2 hours. Place a cooked patty on a slice of bread and top with pickles and condiments. Cover with another piece of bread. Repeat these steps for the second sandwich, and then break out your favorite chips and a drink.

Try not to become a man of success but a man of value.
– Albert Einstein

Zee Mack Patty #2

Ingredients
1 (3.5 oz.) package mackerel
2 (1.3 oz.) jalapeno peppers (singles)
4 sour cream and onion crackers from 1 (1.375 oz.) package
1 (2 oz.) package cream cheese
4 slices bread
ketchup to taste

Directions
Drain most of the juice from the mackerel. Dice jalapeno peppers and crush crackers. Using a large spread bowl, combine mackerel, jalapeno peppers, crackers, and cream cheese. Mix well and divide into 2 equal parts, and form into patties. Place both patties in a clean rice bag and heat in a hot pot for 2 hours. Place a cooked patty on bread and top with ketchup. Cover with another slice of bread and repeat for a second sandwich. Grab those chips and a drink, kick back, and enjoy this one.

To climb steep hills requires a slow pace at first.
– William Shakespeare

Fine Dining Prison Cookbook 2

Zee Mack Patty #3

Ingredients
2 (1.3 oz.) jalapeno peppers (singles)
1/2 (2.75 oz.) bag pork skins
1 (3.5 oz.) package mackerel
1 package chili Ramen seasoning
1 tablespoon hot water
1 (1.375 oz.) package Cheese & Chive crackers
4 slices bread
salad dressing to taste

Directions
Do not drain the mackerel. Dice jalapeno peppers and crush pork skins lightly. Using a large spread bowl, combine mackerel, jalapeno peppers, pork skins, seasoning, and 1 tablespoon hot water. Mix well. Now, crush crackers and add to the bowl. Mix again. Divide the mixture into 2 equal parts and form patties. Place both patties in a clean rice bag and heat in a hot pot for 2 hours. Place a cooked patty on a slice of bread and top with salad dressing. Cover with another piece of bread. Repeat these steps with the other patty. Enjoy this meal with chips and a cold drink.

Your labor is the contribution to this miracle.
– Elizabeth Gilbert

Section 8:
Ham & Spam Dishes

Pork Facts & History

Wikipedia

Pork is the culinary name for meat from a domestic pig (*Sus scrofa domesticus*). It is the most commonly consumed meat worldwide, with evidence of pig husbandry dating back to 5000 BC. Pork is eaten both freshly cooked and preserved. Curing extends the shelf life of the pork products. Ham, smoked pork, gammon, bacon, and sausage are examples of preserved pork. Charcuterie is the branch of cooking devoted to prepared meat products, many from pork.

Pork is the most popular meat in Eastern and Southeastern Asia, and is also very common in the Western world, especially in Central Europe. It is highly prized in Asian cuisines for its fat content and pleasant texture. Consumption of pork is forbidden by Jewish, Muslim, and Rastafarian dietary law, for religious reasons, with several suggested possible causes. The sale of pork is limited in Israel and illegal in certain Muslim countries.

History

Charcuterie is the branch of cooking devoted to prepared meat products such as bacon, ham, sausage, terrines, galantines, pates, and confit, primarily from pork. Originally intended as a way to preserve meat before the advent of refrigeration, these preparations are prepared today for the flavors that are derived from the preservation processes. In 15th-century France, local guilds regulated tradesmen in the food production industry in each city. The guilds that produced charcuterie were those of the charcutiers. The members of this guild produced a traditional range of cooked or salted and dried meats, which varied, sometimes distinctively, from region to region. The only "raw" meat the charcutiers were allowed to sell was unrendered lard. The charcutier prepared numerous items, including pates, rillettes, sausage, bacon, trotters, and head cheese.

Before the mass production and re-engineering of pork in the 20th century, pork in Europe and North America was traditionally an autumn dish – pigs and other livestock coming to the slaughter in the autumn after growing in the spring and fattening during the summer. Due to the seasonal nature of the meat in Western culinary history, apples (harvested in late summer and autumn) have been a staple pairing with fresh pork. The year-round availability of meat and fruits has not diminished the popularity of this combination on Western plates.

Consumption Patterns

Pork is the most widely eaten meat in the world, accounting for about 38% of meat production worldwide. Consumption varies widely from place to place. The meat is taboo to eat in the Middle East and most of the Muslim world because of Jewish kosher and Islamic Halal dietary restrictions. But pork is widely consumed in East and Southeast Asia, Europe, Sub-Saharan Africa, the Americas, and Oceania. As a result, large numbers of pork recipes are developed throughout the world. Jamon is the most famous Spanish ham, which is made with the front legs of a pig. Feijoada, for example, the national dish of Brazil (also served in Portugal), is traditionally prepared with pork trimmings: ears, tail, and feet.

According to the USDA's Foreign Agriculture Service, nearly 100 million metric tons of pork were consumed worldwide in 2006 (preliminary data). Increasing urbanization and disposable income have led to a rapid rise in pork consumption in China, where in 2006 consumption was 20% higher than in 2002, and a further 5% increase is projected in 2007. In 2015, a total of 109.905 million metric tons of pork were consumed worldwide. By 2017, half the world's pork was consumed in China.

Asian Pork Consumption

Pork is popular throughout eastern Asia and the Pacific, where whole roast pig is a popular item in the Pacific Island cuisine. It is consumed in a great many ways and is highly esteemed in Chinese cuisine. Currently, China is the world's largest pork consumer, with pork consumption expected to total 53 million tons in 2012, which accounts for more than half of global pork consumption. In China, pork is preferred over beef for economic and aesthetic reasons; the pig is easy to feed and is not used for labor. The colors of the meat and the fat of pork are regarded as more appetizing, while the taste and smell are described as sweeter and cleaner. It is also considered easier to digest.

In rural tradition, pork is shared to celebrate important occasions and to form bonds. In China, pork is so important that the nation maintains a "strategic pork reserve." Red braised pork (*hong shao rou*), a delicacy from Hunan Province, inspired Mao Zedong. Other popular Chinese pork dishes are sweet and sour pork, *bakkwa*, and *chariu*. In the Philippines, due to 300 years of Spanish colonization and influence, *lechon*, which is an
The entire roasted suckling pig is the national delicacy.

Pork Products

Pork may be cooked from fresh meat or cured over time. Cured meat products include ham and bacon. The carcass may be used in many different ways for fresh meat cuts, with the popularity of certain cuts and certain carcass proportions varying worldwide.

Fresh Meat

Most of the carcass can be used to produce fresh meat, and in the case of a suckling pig, the whole body of a young pig, ranging in age from two to six weeks, is roasted. Danish roast pork or *flæskesøg, prepared with crispy crackling,* is a national favorite as the traditional Christmas dinner.

Processed Pork

Pork is particularly common as an ingredient in sausages. Many traditional European sausages are made with pork, including *chorizo*, *fuet*, Cumberland sausage, and salami. Many brands of American sausages are made from pork. Processing of pork into sausage and other products in France is described as *charcuterie*.

Ham and bacon are made from fresh pork by curing with salt (pickling) or smoking. Shoulders and legs are most commonly cured in this manner for Picnic shoulder and ham, whereas streaky and round bacon comes from the belly.

Ham and bacon are popular foods in the West, and their consumption has increased with industrialization. Non-Western cuisines also use preserved meat products. For example, salted preserved pork or red roasted pork is used in China and Asian cuisine.

Bacon is defined as any of certain cuts of meat taken from the sides, belly, or back that have been cured or smoked. In continental Europe, it is used primarily in cubes (*lardons*) as a cooking ingredient valued both as a source of fat and for its flavor. In Italy, besides being used in cooking, bacon (*pancetta*) is also served uncooked and thinly sliced as part of an antipasto. Bacon is also used for barding roast, especially game birds. Bacon is often smoked with various wood fuels for up to ten hours. Bacon is eaten fried, baked, or grilled.

A side of bacon is a "flitch" or "slab bacon," while an individual slice of bacon is a "rasher" (Australia, Ireland, New Zealand, and the United Kingdom) or simply a "slice" or "strip" (North America). Slices of bacon are also known as "collops." Traditionally, the skin is left cut and is known as "bacon rind." Rindless bacon, however, is quite common. In both Ireland and the United Kingdom, bacon comes in a wide variety of cuts and flavors, and is predominantly known as "streaky bacon" or "streaky rashers." Bacon made from the meat on the back of the pig is referred to as "back bacon" and is part of a traditional full breakfast commonly eaten in Britain and Ireland. In the United States, back bacon may also be referred to as "Canadian-style Bacon" or "Canadian Bacon."

The USDA defines bacon as "the cured belly of a swine carcass," while other cuts and characteristics must be separately qualified (e.g., "smoked pork loin bacon"). "USDA Certified," bacon means that it has been treated for Trichinella.

Industrial Raw Material

Due to the fact that pigs can eat unused food originally meant for humans, and due to the high availability of such food in many industrialized countries, pork and other products from pigs have become securely sourced and low-priced commodities. That makes pig products very popular as raw material in many industrially produced products.

Fine Dining's Ham-Mac & Cheese

Ingredients
1 (1.3 oz.) jalapeno pepper (single)
1 (3 oz.) chicken Ramen noodles
2 (3 oz.) packages Spam
1/2 teaspoon salt
1/4 coffee mug salad dressing
1/2 coffee mug squeeze cheese
1/2 sleeve saltine crackers
1 1/2 coffee mugs hot water
1 teaspoon black pepper
1 package chicken Ramen seasoning

Directions
Dice the jalapeno pepper and Spam into fairly small pieces. In a large spread bowl, combine Ramen and hot water. Cover the bowl tightly and steep for 5 minutes. Drain any remaining water and rinse noodles in cold water. Now, set aside saltine crackers and combine all ingredients into a spread bowl. Mix well. That's it. Look out, Kraft, you have some competition. This is a perfect meal for one. Eat with your saltines or sub with tortilla chips.

The talent of success is nothing more than doing what you can do, well.
– Henry W. Longfellow

Troy Traylor

Pineapple; Spam & Rice

Ingredients
1/4 (8 oz.) bag instant white rice
1 1/2 coffee mugs hot water
1 (3 oz.) package Spam
1 filling from (4 oz.) cherry pie
1 (4 oz.) serving pineapples from tray

Directions
In a large spread bowl combine rice and hot water. Cover the bowl tightly and steep for 10 minutes. While waiting, dice Spam into fairly small pieces and remove the cherry filling from the pie. Drain all juices from the pineapples. Now, drain the remaining water from the rice and combine all ingredients and mix well. Put all in a large chip bag, double bag, and cook in a hot pot for 1 hour. Once cooked, put all in a large spread bowl and eat up. This is a meal to enjoy.

Impatience never commanded success.
– Edwin H. Chapin

Spam Cheeseburgers

Ingredients
1 (3 oz.) package of Spam
2 (1.3 oz.) jalapeno peppers (singles)
1/2 (9 oz.) dill pickle (any flavor)
1/2 (11 oz.) bag cheese puffs
3 tablespoons salad dressing
6 slices bread
a pinch of black pepper
a pinch of salt

Directions
Dice jalapeno peppers. Slice pickles as you would for a burger. Crush cheese puffs and dice Spam into small pieces. In a spread bowl, combine Spam, cheese puffs, jalapeno pepper pieces, and knead well. Divide the mixture into 3 equal parts. Form patties out of this mixture. Using 3 rice bags, place one patty in each bag and heat in a hot pot for 2 hours. Once cooked, remove patties from the hot pot and place 1 each on a slice of bread. Top each with a pickle, salt, pepper, and salad dressing. Cover each with a second piece of bread. Enjoy these burgers with your favorite side.

If you wish success in life, make perseverance your bosom friend, experience your wise counselor, caution your elder brother, and hope your guardian genius.
– Joseph Addison

Spam & Cheese Sandwich

Ingredients
1/4 (9 oz.) dill pickle (any flavor)
2 tablespoons squeeze cheese
1 heaping tablespoon salad dressing
2 slices bread
1 (3 oz.) package Spam

Directions
Slice the pickle as you would for a burger. Spread cheese and salad dressing on your bread. Place Spam on top and cover with pickle. Now top with the remaining piece of bread. Can bag and heat in a hot pot or eat chilled – either way is just as delicious. Grab chips and a drink and enjoy!

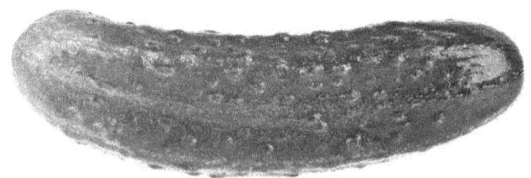

My message to you is simple, keep believing, keep marching, keep building, and keep raising your voice. – Barack Obama

Spam Salad

Ingredients
1 (3 oz.) package Spam
1 teaspoon onion flakes
1/4 (9 oz.) pickle (any flavor)
1 heaping tablespoon salad dressing
1/4 teaspoon garlic powder
2 hard-boiled eggs
1 tablespoon hot water
1/2 tablespoon relish
1/2 teaspoon black pepper

Directions
Dice Spam and eggs. Set eggs aside for a moment. Hydrate the onion flakes with the tablespoon of hot water. Combine all ingredients except eggs in a spread bowl and mix well. Now add eggs to this and lightly mix again. Eat on bread, saltine crackers, or tortilla chips. Don't be afraid to add a shot of squeeze cheese.

Success is the good fortune that comes from aspiration, desperation, perspiration, and inspiration.
– Evan Esar

Helpful Cooking Tips

When mincing garlic, sprinkle on a little salt so the pieces won't stick to your knife or cutting board.

If your cake recipe calls for nuts, heat them first in the oven, then dust them with flour before adding them to the batter to keep them from settling to the bottom of the pan.

Noodles, spaghetti, and other starches won't boil over if you rub the inside of the pot with vegetable oil.

Brown gravy in a hurry with a bit of instant coffee straight from the jar ... no bitter taste, either.

For a juicier hamburger, add cold water to the beef before grilling (1/2 cup to 1 pound of meat).

To keep cauliflower white while cooking, add a little milk to the water.

Let raw potatoes stand in cold water for at least half an hour before frying to improve the crispness of French-fried potatoes.

Use a gentle touch when shaping ground beef patties. Over-handling will result in a firm, compact texture after cooking. Don't press or flatten with a spatula during cooking.

Never heat pesto sauce; the basil will turn black and taste bitter.

Butter pie pastry scraps: sprinkle with cinnamon and sugar and bake like cookies.

When slicing a hard-boiled egg, try wetting the knife just before cutting. If that doesn't do the trick, try applying a bit of cooking spray to the edge.

Microwave a lemon for 15 seconds and double the juice you get before squeezing.

Microwave garlic cloves for 15 seconds, and the skins slip right off.

Section 9:
Mexican Dishes

Troy Traylor

Fabulous Frito Pie

Ingredients
1 (16 oz.) bag corn chips
2 (8 oz.) packages Mexican beef
1 (3.5 oz.) package pepperoni slices
2 (2 oz.) packages cream cheese
1 (2 oz.) package ranch dressing
1 (11.25 oz.) package chili no beans
3 (1.3 oz.) jalapeno peppers (singles)
1/2 (16 oz.) bag tortilla chips
1/4 (16 oz.) bottle squeeze cheese
2 1/4 coffee mugs hot water
5 tablespoons onion flakes
1 coffee mug refried beans
1/4 coffee mug salsa

Directions
Crush corn chips and carefully add hot water to the bag while kneading into a pliable dough. Keep the dough moist enough so all the ingredients stick together, but not too wet. Use no more than a 1/4 of a coffee mug. Place the dough into a large spread bowl and work  into a pie crust. Smooth out when done. Place the bowl under a fan to dry for 2 hours. While the crust is drying, combine refried beans and 2 coffee mugs of hot water in a large spread bowl. Cover the bowl tightly and steep for 10 minutes. Using a large chip bag, combine refried beans, chili no beans, Mexican beef, salsa, and onion flakes. Double bag for safety. Heat the bag in a hot pot while the crust is drying. Stir occasionally. You may need to add a little water to keep it moist. When the crust is ready,

dice jalapeno peppers and pepperoni slices into small pieces. Coat your crust with cream cheese. Crush tortilla chips lightly. Spoon half the bean mixture into the crust, half the tortilla chips, and half the pepper and pepperoni pieces. Top with squeeze cheese. Repeat this process again and top off with ranch dressing. Let this sit for 30 minutes to stiffen up. You should be able to cut this like a pie. This is just fabulous!

Life isn't about waiting for the storm to pass... it's learning to dance in the rain.
– Vivian Greene

Hearty Nachos

Ingredients
1 (8 oz.) package Mexican or ground beef
1/4 (16 oz.) bottle squeeze cheese
1/4 (16 oz.) bag tortillas chips
1/4 coffee mug salsa
3 (1.3 oz.) jalapeno peppers (singles)

Directions
Rinse off the meat package and open it. Add salsa and squeeze cheese into the package. Heat the package in a hot pot for 1 hour. Stir occasionally. While waiting, dice jalapeno peppers. Once the meat package is hot, layer the bowl with tortilla chips and cover with the meat mixture. Repeat until the mixture is exhausted. Now decorate with pepper pieces. Makes a great quick snack on a rainy day.

*Only those who will risk going too far
can possibly find out how far one can go.
– T.S. Eliot*

Insider Burladas

Ingredients
5 (11.25 oz.) packages chili no beans
1 (8 oz.) package Mexican or ground beef
3 1/2 coffee mugs hot water
1 (18 oz.) box cheese nips
2 (10 oz.) packages flour tortillas
1 (15 oz.) bottle chili con queso
2 (11.25 oz) packages chili with beans
1 1/2 coffee mugs refried beans
1/2 (8 oz.) bag jalapeno chips
1/2 (2.75 oz.) bag pork skins
6 (1.3 oz.) jalapeno peppers (singles)
1 coffee mug salsa

Directions
You will need 3 hot pots and several spread bowls. Rinse meat packages and heat in a hot pot for 30 minutes. Using a large spread bowl, combine refried beans and hot water. Cover the bowl tightly and steep for 10 minutes. Using a separate bowl, crush jalapeno chips and cheese nips. Spoon in 3 to 4 tablespoons of water and begin mixing well. Slowly add in up to 1 1/2 more tablespoons of water and continue to mix into a thick paste. Remove the Mexican beef and chili with beans from the hot pots and pour into the refried beans. Crush pork skins and add to this mixture. Mix well. Now

coat each flour tortilla with the paste and the chili con queso. Spoon bean mixture onto tortillas and roll. Grab several rice bags. Place 4 burritos in each rice bag and heat in a hot pot for 2 hours. Dice jalapeno peppers into small pieces. Remove rice bags from hot pots and put 4 in each bowl. Cover each bowl with chili without beans and drizzle with more chili con queso. Now decorate each bowl with pepper pieces and top with salsa. Repeat these steps with the remaining mixture. Will feed 5 hungry people, for sure. Burrito + Enchilada = Burladas. If Cheese Nips are not available at your unit, substitute with Cheese Puffs.

> *To reach a port, we must sail, sometimes with the wind, and sometimes against it. But we must not drift or lie at anchor.*
> *– Oliver Wendell Holmes*

Killer Frito Pie

Ingredients
1 (11.25 oz.) package chili with beans
1/4 (8 oz.) bottle habanera sauce
1 coffee mug refried beans
1 (16 oz.) bag corn chips
1/2 (16 oz.) bottle squeeze cheese
3 (1.3 oz.) jalapeno peppers (singles)
2 coffee mugs hot water

Directions
Rinse the chili package, open it, and add the squeeze cheese and habanero sauce. Heat the package in a hot pot for 30 minutes. Stir occasionally. You may need to add 3 or so tablespoons of water to this as you stir. While waiting, dice jalapeno peppers. You can add them to the chili package now or after it's cooked. In a large spread bowl, combine refried beans and hot water. Cover tightly and steep for 10 minutes. Once the chili is hot, pour it into the refried beans. Using another bowl, layer with 1/3 of the chips and top with 1/3 of the bean mixture. Repeat these steps 2 more times. Grab your favorite drink and relax. It is time to eat.

At the end of the day it's not about what you have or even what you've accomplished ... it's about who you've lifted up, who you've made better; it's about what you've given back.
– Denzel Washington

Troy Traylor

Loaded and Coated Burritos

Ingredients
1/2 coffee mug instant white rice
2 coffee mugs hot water
2 (1.3 oz.) jalapeno peppers (singles)
8 flour tortillas
1 (2 oz.) package ranch dressing
1/2 coffee mug refried beans
1 (11.25 oz.) package chili with beans
1 good handful jalapeno chips
1/4 (16 oz.) bottle squeeze cheese
1 coffee mug cheese puffs
Habanero sauce to taste

Directions
You will need 2 hot pots and 2 large spread bowls. In a large spread bowl, combine rice, refried beans, and hot water. Mix well, cover bowl tightly, and steep for 10 minutes. While waiting, rinse the meat package and heat it in a hot pot for 30 minutes. Dice jalapeno peppers and crush the chips while this heats. Once the meat package is hot, pour it into the refried bean mixture and add pepper pieces and chips. Stir well. Now separate flour tortillas and coat all with cheese. Spoon mixture onto tortillas and roll up. Place 4 burritos into a rice bag and cook in separate hot pots for 2 hours. Once done, place 4 in each spread bowl and top with ranch dressing. Now, crush cheese puffs and cover. Sprinkle on habanero and you're ready for a real treat. Enjoy!

The secret of success in life is for a man to be ready for his opportunity when it comes.
– Earl of Beaconsfield

Maryland Menudo

Ingredients

1/2 (8 oz.) bag instant white rice
1 coffee mug crushed tortilla chips
2 coffee mugs hot water
1 (3 oz.) package Spam
1 (9 oz.) pickle (any flavor)
1 (12 oz.) V-8 juice
3 tablespoons onion flakes
1 tablespoon garlic powder
2 (2.75 oz.) bags pork skins
2 tablespoons hot sauce of choice
3 tablespoons pickle juice
2 packages beef Ramen seasonings
2 (4 oz.) servings mixed vegetables from tray
1 (4 oz.) serving corn from tray
1 (6 oz.) package corn nuts

Directions

You will need 2 hot pots and several large spread bowls. In 1 spread bowl, combine the rice with 1 1/4 coffee mugs hot water. Cover the bowl tightly and steep for 10 minutes. At the same time, rice is cooking, crush tortilla chips, place in another bowl, and spread with a light 1/4 coffee mug of hot water. Knead this into the dough. When rice is done, add it to the dough mixture and knead again. Place this mixture into a clean chip bag, that bag in another bag, and heat in a hot pot for 30 minutes. While heating, dice the Spam and pickle into small pieces. In another spread bowl, combine Spam, pickle, V-8 juice, onion flakes, and garlic powder. Mix well. Pour this mixture into a rice bag and place it in another hot pot for 30 minutes. While waiting, place pork skins into a spread bowl and add just enough hot water to hydrate thoroughly. Once everything is cooked, combine all mixtures and remaining ingredients and mix well. This one is simply incredible.

My Gumbo

Ingredients
1 (5 oz.) summer sausage
1 (3.5 oz.) package mackerel
1 (7 oz.) package chicken chunks
1/2 (2.75 oz.) bag pork skins
2 (1.3 oz.) jalapeno peppers (singles)
1 (12 oz.) V-8 juice
1 package chili Ramen seasoning
1/4 (8 oz.) bag instant white rice
3/4 coffee mug hot water

Directions
Dice summer sausage into small pieces. Drain the mackerel and chicken chunks. Lightly crush pork skins and dice jalapeno peppers into small pieces. In a large chip bag, combine all ingredients, mix well, and double bag, then heat in a hot pot for 4 hours. Stir occasionally. If this begins to dry out, just add a little water. This is a super-good meal. Enjoy!

*If you think, then you will be prepared.
If you are prepared, then you will have no worries.
– Li Ka Shing*

Troy Traylor

My Menudo #1

Ingredients
1/4 (16 oz.) bag tortilla chips
1/4 (8 oz.) bag instant white rice
2 1/4 coffee mugs hot water
1 (5 oz.) summer sausage (can sub with Spam)
1 (11.25 oz.) package chili no beans
2 packages chili Ramen seasoning
3 (2.75 oz.) bags pork skins
1/2 (9 oz.) pickle (any flavor)
3 tablespoons pickle juice

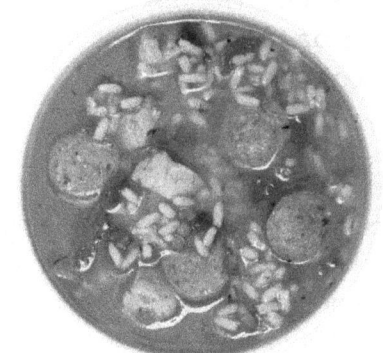

Directions
Crush tortilla chips and place in a large spread bowl. In a separate spread bowl combine instant rice and hot water. Cover the bowl tightly and steep for 10 minutes. Add tortilla chips to the rice bowl with a 1/4 cup of hot water and knead into a dough. Place the dough into a clean plastic bag, double-bag it, and heat in a hot pot for 30 minutes. While waiting, dice summer sausage or Spam into small pieces. In a spread bowl, combine the sausage or Spam, chili no beans, seasoning packages, and 1 cup hot water. Cover for a moment. Lightly crush pork skins and add to chili bowl. Mix well. You want the pork skins to hydrate. Dice the pickle into small pieces. Now, combine all mixtures in 1 bowl and mix well. Serve it up!

Success does not consist in never making blunders, but in never making the same one a second time.
– Josh Billings

Fine Dining Prison Cookbook 2

Nachos #1

Ingredients
1 (11.25 oz.) package chili no beans
1 (11.25 oz.) package chili with beans
1 (3 oz.) chili Ramen noodles
1 coffee mug refried beans
3 coffee mugs hot water
1 (9 oz.) pickle (any flavor)
6 (1.3 oz.) jalapeno peppers (singles)
1 (16 oz.) bag tortilla chips
1/2 (16 oz.) bottle squeeze cheese
1 (2 oz.) package ranch dressing
hot sauce of choice to taste

Directions
Rinse both meat packages off and heat in a hot pot. In a large spread bowl, combine Ramen, refried beans, and hot water. Cover tightly and steep for 10 minutes. While waiting, dice the pickle and jalapeno peppers into small pieces. Once the meat packages are hot, pour them into the bean mixture and stir well in a separate bowl, layer with tortilla chips, and top with bean mixture, cheese, pickle, and pepper pieces. Repeat this process until the mixture is gone. Top it off with ranch dressing and hot sauce. I hope you're hungry.

I cannot give you the formula for success, but I can give you the formula for failure – which is: Try to please everybody.
– Herbert Bayard Swope

Nachos #2

Ingredients
2 (11.25 oz.) packages chili with beans
2 coffee mugs hot water
1 (16 oz.) bag tortilla chips
1 (2 oz.) package ranch dressing
2 tablespoons pickle juice
1 coffee mug refried beans
2 (1.3 oz.) jalapeno peppers (singles)
2 (3 oz.) bags nacho chips
1/2 (16 oz.) bottle squeeze cheese

Directions
Rinse the meat packages off and heat in a hot pot for 30 minutes. In a large spread bowl, combine refried beans and hot water. Cover bowl tightly and steep for 10 minutes. While waiting, dice jalapeno peppers into small pieces. Once the meat packages are hot, pour them into the refried bean mixture. Add jalapeno pieces to the bowl and mix well. In a separate bowl, layer the bowl with tortilla chips and nacho chips. Top with bean mixture. Repeat until all the mixture and chips are gone. Top this with ranch dressing, cheese, and pickle juice. You cannot eat just one.

> *If you take risk and face your fate with dignity, there is nothing you can do that makes you small: if you don't take risk there is nothing you can do that makes you grand, nothing.*
> *– Nicholas Taleb*

Tasty Tacos

Ingredients
2 (1.3 oz.) jalapeno peppers (singles)
1 (3 oz.) bag Cheetos
1 (8 oz.) package beef tips
1 (8 oz.) bag regular potato chips
1 (10 oz.) package flour tortillas
1/4 (16 oz.) bottle squeeze cheese
3/4 coffee mug refried beans
2 coffee mugs hot water
1 packet chili Ramen seasoning
Habanero sauce to taste

Directions
Dice jalapeno peppers into small pieces and crush chips. Set flour tortillas aside. In a large clean chip bag, combine the remaining ingredients and mix well. Double bag. Heat the bag in a hot pot for 1 hour, then spoon the mixture onto flour tortillas and fold in half. Place 4 tacos in a rice bag and heat in a hot pot for an additional hour. Once done, grab a cold drink and enjoy. This is one meal to enjoy.

Everyone has a fair turn to be as great as he pleases.
– Jeremy Collier

Tasty Tostitos

Ingredients
2 (1.3 oz.) jalapeno peppers (singles)
1 (8 oz.) package Mexican beef
1 (16 oz.) bag corn chips
3 (2 oz.) packages cream cheese
1/4 (12 oz.) bottle salsa (12 tablespoons)
1/4 coffee mug hot water

Directions
Dice jalapeno peppers. In a large spread bowl, combine pepper pieces, cream cheese, Mexican beef, and salsa. Mix well. Crush corn chips in the bag and slowly add the hot water as you knead into pliable dough. You do not want it too wet, just moist enough so it sticks together. Flatten the dough out in a bag like a pizza. Cut open the bag and, using your ID card, cut the dough into 6" x 8" squares. Spoon a little mixture onto each square and roll up. Once all are rolled up, place 6 or so at a time in a rice bag and cook in a hot pot for 2 1/2 hours. Once they are cooked, place them in your spread bowl and top with cheese or more salsa. Don't be afraid to be creative.

The difference between a successful person and others is not a lack of knowledge, but rather a lack of will.
– Vince Lombardi

Texas-Penn Tamales

Ingredients
2 (8 oz.) packages Mexican beef
1 (12 oz.) V-8 juice
1/2 (16 oz.) bottle squeeze cheese
3/4 coffee mug refried beans
1 (10 oz.) package flour tortillas
1/2 (12 oz.) bottle salsa

Directions
In a large, clean chip bag, combine Mexican beef, refried beans, and the can of V-8 juice. Double bag and heat in a hot pot for 1 hour. At the same time, this is cooking, separate flour tortillas and spread some cheese on each. Remove the mixture from the hot pot and spoon some mixture on each. Do not make these too thick. Roll each up and place 6 in a rice bag. Place the bag in a hot pot to heat for 45 minutes. Once done, place all in a spread bowl and top with salsa. You can add some peppers to these as well.

What lies behind us and what lies before us are tiny matters compared to what lies within us.
– Henry Stanley Haskins

The Ultimate Burritos

Ingredients
3 (1.3 oz.) jalapeno peppers (singles)
1 (6 oz.) bag Salsa Verde chips
2 (2.75 oz.) bags pork skins
3 (11.25 oz.) packages chili no beans
2 (11.25 oz.) packages pot roast
2 packages chili Ramen seasoning
1/2 (16 oz.) bottle squeeze cheese
1 (12 oz.) spicy or regular V-8 juice
1 1/2 coffee mugs refried beans
1/2 coffee mug hot water
1 (10 oz.) package flour tortillas
1/2 (11 oz.) bag cheese puffs

Directions
You will need 4 hot pots for this recipe. Dice the jalapeno peppers and crush the Salsa Verde chips and pork skins. In a large chip bag, combine all the ingredients except 1 chili, no beans, flour tortillas, and cheese puffs. Knead this well. Tie up and allow all liquids to absorb. Stir well once absorbed. Place this mixture in a large spread bowl or two. Spoon mixture onto flour tortillas and roll. Exhaust the mixed ingredients. Using rice bags, place 4 burritos in each bag. Place one bag in each hot pot and cook for 2 hours. Once cooked, place 4 burritos each in 4 separate spread bowls. Open the last chili no beans and pour over the top of each bowl. Crush cheese puffs and top each burrito. You can add hot sauce, but you really don't need it.

*Failures do what is tension relieving,
while winners do what is goal achieving.
– Dennis Waitley*

Helpful Cooking Tips

A Perfect Pastry Crust? In your favorite recipe, substitute a 4:1 ratio of lard with butter.

It's important to let a roast beef, pork, lamb, or poultry sit a little while before carving. That allows the juices to retreat back into the meat. If you carve a roast too soon, much of its goodness will spill out onto the carving board.

Avoid using metal bowls when mixing salads. Use wooden, glass, or china.

Sausage patties rolled in flour before frying won't crack open during cooking.

Two drops of yellow food coloring added to boiling noodles will make them look homemade.

When separating eggs, break them into a funnel. The whites will go through, leaving the yolk intact in the funnel.

When tossing a salad with a basic vinaigrette, always make the vinaigrette at least 1/2 hour ahead of time and let the mixture sit to allow the flavors to marry. Pour the vinaigrette down the side of the bowl, not directly on the greens, for a more evenly dressed salad.

For the perfect boiled egg, cover eggs with cold water and a pinch of salt. Bring the water to a full boil. Remove the pan from the heat and cover. Let the eggs sit for 8-9 minutes. Drain the water and place the eggs in ice water to cool to stop the cooking process.

When braising meat, cook it at a low temperature for a long time to keep the meat tender and retain all the juices.

When cooking any kind of strawberry dessert, add a splash of aged Balsamic vinegar to the recipe to enhance the flavor of the strawberries.

Troy Traylor

Section 10:
Pizzas

Troy Traylor

Big House Spicy Pizza

Ingredients
1 (11.25 oz.) package chili with beans
1/4 (16 oz.) bag corn chips
3/4 coffee mug refried beans
5 coffee mugs hot water
3 (1.3 oz.) jalapeno peppers (singles)
1/4 (8 oz.) bag jalapeno chips
1/4 (16 oz.) bottle squeeze cheese
3 (3 oz.) chili Ramen noodles
1 (6 oz.) bag Salsa Verde chips
1/4 (8 oz.) bag instant white rice
1 package chili Ramen seasoning
1 (9 oz.) pickle (any flavor)
1/4 (14 oz.) jar salad dressing

Directions
You will need 2 hot pots and some newspaper. Rinse off the meat package and heat it in a hot pot for 1 hour. Crush Ramen and all chips. Using a large chip bag, combine Ramen, corn, and Salsa Verde chips, refried beans, rice, the 1 chili Ramen seasoning, and hot water. Knead the mixture into a pliable dough. Flatten out the mixture in a chip bag and wrap in a newspaper. Set aside. Dice jalapeno peppers and pickle. Once the meat packages have cooked, unwrap the pizza crust and cover with salad dressing. Remove the meat package from the hot pot and evenly spread it over the pizza. Now cover with pepper pieces, pickle, jalapeno chips, and top with squeeze cheese. This is an incredibly good meal!

Did you know? Americans love pizza so much that we eat about 100 acres of pizza every day, 350 slices every second, according to the National Association of Pizza operators.

Fine Dining Prison Cookbook 2

Hawaiian Pizza

Ingredients
2 (11.25 oz.) packages chili with beans
1/4 (16 oz.) bag corn chips
3 (3 oz.) Ramen noodles (any flavor)
1/2 (9 oz.) pickle
1/4 (16 oz.) bottle squeeze cheese
2 coffee mugs fruit cocktail juice
1 coffee mug refried beans
1 1/4 coffee mugs hot water
3 (1.3 oz.) jalapeno peppers (singles)
1 coffee mug fruit cocktail from tray (no juice)

Directions
You will need 2 hot pots, 1 rice bag, and newspaper. Rinse meat packages and heat in a hot pot for 1 hour. Pour fruit cocktail juice in a rice bag and place in the second hot pot for 45 minutes. While waiting, crush corn chips and Ramen. In a large chip bag, combine corn chips, refried beans, and Ramen. Shake well and set aside. Once the juice in the second pot has heated for 45 minutes, pour it and the hot water into the chip bag and knead the mixture into pliable dough. Flatten out in a chip bag and wrap in a newspaper. Set aside for 20 minutes. Dice the pickle and jalapeno peppers. Once the meat and dough are ready, cut open the dough and cover with squeeze cheese. Evenly spread the meat packages over the top. Now you can decorate pizza with pickles, pepper pieces, and fruit cocktail. Grab a cold drink and enjoy every bite. Probably need help from the kitchen for fruit cocktail and juice.

Did you know? Nobody knows how the word pizza originated. The word pizza was first documented around 997 AD in Gaeta, Italy. After that the name started to spread to different parts of central and southern Italy.

Meat Lover's Pizza

Ingredients

1 (5 oz.) summer sausage
1 (11. 25 oz.) package chili no beans
1/2 (16 oz.) bag corn chips
1 (9 oz.) dill pickle
1/2 (8 oz.) bag jalapeno chips
1/2 coffee mug ketchup
1 (8 oz.) package Mexican/ground beef
3 (3 oz.) chili Ramen noodles
1 coffee mug refried beans
2 packages chili Ramen seasoning
4 (1.3 oz.) jalapeno peppers (singles)
1/2 (16 oz.) bottle squeeze cheese
3 3/4 coffee mugs hot water
hot sauce to taste

Directions

You will need 2 hot pots and a newspaper. Dice the summer sausage and rinse off the meat packages. Open the meat packages and put all the summer sausage pieces in them. Heat meat packages in a hot pot for 1 hour. While waiting, crush Ramen and corn chips. In the chip bag, combine Ramen, refried beans, and hot water. Knead until the water absorbs. Flatten out in a chip bag and wrap in a newspaper. Set aside. While waiting, dice the pickle, jalapeno peppers, and crush the chips. Once everything is cooked, cut open the chip bag and spread cheese evenly. Remove meat packages from the hot pot and combine all in one package. Mix well. Now spread this over the pizza evenly. Sprinkle the 2 seasoning packages over the pizza. Now decorate with pickles, peppers, and chips. Drizzle ketchup and hot sauce over the top. Cut and serve. You will love every bite. Cook time for the Ramen mixture is 20 minutes.

Player's Pizza

Ingredients
2 (3.5 oz.) packages mackerel
2 (11.25 oz.) packages chili no beans
4 (1.3 oz.) jalapeno peppers (singles)
1/2 (9 oz.) pickle (any flavor)
2 (5 oz.) summer sausages
1 (12 oz.) V-8 juice
3 (3 oz.) chili Ramen noodles
3/4 coffee mug refried beans
1 (2.75 oz.) bag pork skins
1 (6 oz.) bag Salsa Verde chips
1 package chili Ramen seasoning
2 1/2 coffee mugs hot water
1/4 (16 oz.) bottle squeeze cheese
1 (3 oz.) bag nacho chips
2 (2 oz.) packages ranch dressing
hot sauce to taste

Directions
You will need 1 rice bag, 1 large cheese puffs bag, newspaper, 2 hot pots, and a few spread bowls. Drain mackerel. Rinse chili packages and open. Mix one package of mackerel into each chili package. Place chili packages in a hot pot to heat for 1 hour. Dice jalapeno peppers, pickle, and summer sausage. Combine summer sausage pieces and V-8 juice in the rice bag and place in a hot pot to heat for 45 minutes. While waiting, crush Ramen, pork skins, and Salsa Verde chips. In the cheese puffs bag, combine the Ramen, refried beans, pork skins, Salsa Verde chips, and chili seasoning. Shake well. Remove rice bag from hot pot and drain V-8 juice into Ramen mixture. Add hot water to this, 2 cups to begin with, and knead into pliable dough. Don't allow dough to become too wet. Once kneaded, flatten out the dough in a bag and wrap in old newspaper. Set aside for 15

minutes. Once everything is cooked, cut open the dough and layer in this way: cheese, meat package, summer sausage, pickle, and jalapeno pieces. Crush nacho chips. Sprinkle chips over pizza and cover with ranch dressing and hot sauce. This is a player's pizza, because only true players can flip the bill for this one.

Did you know? In 2001, the Russian Space Agency was paid more than a million bucks to deliver a six-inch pizza to the International Space Station. Russian cosmonaut Yuri Usachov had the honor of being the first person to receive a pizza delivery while in orbit.

Slice of Seafood Pizza

Ingredients
1 (16 oz.) bag corn chips
1 coffee mug refried beans
1 1/4 coffee mugs hot water
2 (1.3 oz.) jalapeno peppers (singles)
1 (12 oz.) V-8 juice
2 (3.5 oz.) packages mackerel
1 (7 oz.) package chicken chunks
1 (4.23 oz.) package tuna
1/2 (3.5 oz.) package (25 slices) pepperoni
1 coffee mug ketchup
1 package shrimp Ramen seasoning
1 teaspoon onion powder
1/2 teaspoon garlic powder
3 tablespoons onion flakes
1 1/2 tablespoons habanero sauce
1/2 (16 oz.) bottle squeeze cheese
1 (3.53 oz.) package sardines
1/2 (11 oz.) bag party mix
1/2 (9 oz.) dill pickle

Directions
You will need 1 rice bag, old newspaper, and 2 hot pots. Prepare the crust. Crush the corn chips in their bag into a fine powder. Add refried beans to the bag with hot water. Knead this into pliable dough. Once kneaded, flatten out the mixture in the chip bag and even it out. Wrap in newspaper and set aside until sauce is ready. Prepare sauce: Dice jalapeno peppers. In a rice bag, combine V-8 juice, mackerel (you can drain if you prefer), chicken chunks, tuna, pepperoni slices, jalapeno pepper pieces, ketchup, shrimp Ramen seasoning, onion and garlic powder, onion flakes, and habanero sauce. Mix well and heat in a hot pot for 2 hours. Once cooked, cut the chip bag open and flatten out

until fairly thin. Spread cheese over the crust. Crush the party mix and dice the pickle. Remove the sauce from the hot pot and pour it over the pizza. Decorate pizza with sardines, party mix, and pickles. This one is a real belt buster.

Did you know? The biggest pizza in recorded history was prepared by Dovilio Nardi, Andrea Mannacchi, Marco Nardi, Matteo Nardi, and Hatteo Giannotte in Rome Italy on December 13, 2012. It had a total surface area of 13,580.28 ft.^{2}. Guinness was on hand to document the massive pie.

Section 11:
Breakfast

Troy Traylor

Breakfast Burritos #1

Ingredients
1/4 (5 oz.) summer sausage
2 (1.3 oz.) jalapeno peppers (singles)
1/2 coffee mug instant potatoes (four cheese is best)
8 tablespoons refried beans
2 1/4 coffee mugs hot water
2 tablespoons onion flakes
4 flour tortillas
4 tablespoons squeeze cheese
1 heaping serving scrambled eggs (about 4 eggs)
1/4 coffee mug salsa
pinch black pepper

Directions
Dice summer sausage and jalapeno peppers into small pieces. In a large, spread bowl, combine instant potatoes, refried beans, hot water, and onion flakes. Mix until potatoes are smooth but thick. Cover flour tortillas with squeeze cheese. Layer with instant potato mixture, summer sausage, jalapeno pepper pieces, scrambled eggs, and black pepper. Top off with salsa and roll into 4 burritos. Place these in a rice bag and heat in a hot pot for 2 hours. Can be covered with additional cheese and salsa if you desire. Incredible!

Success is sweet; the sweeter if long delayed and attained through manifold struggles and defeats.
– A. Branson Alcott

Breakfast Burritos #2

Ingredients
1 (3.5 oz.) package mackerel
1 heaping serving scrambled eggs (about 4 eggs)
4 flour tortillas
4 tablespoons squeeze cheese
1/4 (9 oz.) pickle (any flavor)
8 tablespoons refried beans
9 teaspoons of hot water
4 tablespoons of salsa

Directions
Drain juices from mackerel. Fluff mackerel in a spread bowl, then add eggs and mix well. Coat flour tortillas with squeeze cheese. Dice pickle. In a small bowl, combine refried beans and hot water. Cover for 3 minutes. When refried beans are ready, layer flour tortillas with eggs, pickle, and refried beans. Roll each and place all 4 in a rice bag. Heat the bag in a hot pot for 2 hours. Once cook time is up, place all 4 in a spread bowl and cover with salsa: MMM Good!

Adversity reveals genius, prosperity conceals it.
– Horace

Troy Traylor

Breakfast Burritos #3

Ingredients
1 (8 oz.) package Mexican beef
2 (1.3 oz.) jalapeno peppers (singles)
1/2 coffee mug four cheese instant potatoes
8 tablespoons refried beans
1 1/2 coffee mugs hot water
4 flour tortillas
4 tablespoons squeeze cheese
1 heaping serving scrambled eggs (about 4 eggs)
4 tablespoons salsa
hot sauce to taste

Directions
Rinse the package of Mexican beef and dice jalapeno peppers. Place pepper pieces in the meat package and heat in a hot pot for 1 hour. In a spread bowl combine instant potatoes, refried beans, and hot water. Mix until smooth but stiff. Coat the flour tortillas with squeeze cheese. Once the meat package is hot, add it to the potato mixture, along with scrambled eggs, and mix well. Spoon onto tortillas and top with hot sauce. Roll tortillas and place 4 in a rice bag. Heat the bag in a hot pot for 2 hours. Once cooked, place all in a spread bowl and top with salsa.

Great things are not accomplished by those who yield to trends and fads and popular opinion.
– Jack Kerouac

Breakfast Burritos #4

Ingredients
8 tablespoons refried beans
1 heaping tablespoon onion flakes
4 tablespoons squeeze cheese
4 tablespoons salsa
1/4 coffee mug hot water
4 flour tortillas
1 heaping serving scrambled eggs (about 4 eggs)

Directions
In a small bowl or cup, combine refried beans with most of the hot water. Save a few drops for the onion flakes. Cover the container and steep for 5 minutes. Hydrate onion flakes in a few drops of hot water. Now coat flour tortillas with squeeze cheese and top with eggs, refried beans, and onion flakes. Roll into burritos and place 4 in a rice bag. Heat the bag in a hot pot for 2 hours. Once cooked, place all 4 in a spread bowl and cover with salsa. Very easy and very good meal!

*The greatest thing in the world
is to know how to belong to oneself.
– Michel de Montaigne*

Creamy Oatmeal

Ingredients
1/4 coffee mug instant oatmeal (any flavor)
1/4 coffee mug hot water
2 oatmeal cream pies
1 tablespoon peanut butter

Directions
Combine oatmeal and hot water. Cover bowl and steep 3 minutes. Crush oatmeal cream pies. Combine the remaining ingredients with the oatmeal and mix well. Now it's time to enjoy the best oatmeal ever.

*A failure is a man who has blundered,
but is not able to cash in on the experience.
– Elbert Hubbard*

Fine Dining Prison Cookbook 2

My-Hop Pancakes

Ingredients
1 (2 oz.) package cream cheese
4 tablespoons strawberry preserves or grape jelly
3 pancakes from breakfast tray

Directions
Combine the cream cheese and strawberry preserves (or grape jelly) and mix well. Spread over the pancakes, and you're back in the world. Thanks for choosing My-Hop!

Success is the sum of small efforts, repeated day in and day out.
– Robert Collier

More My-Hop Pancakes

Ingredients
1 (2 oz.) package cream cheese
1 heaping tablespoon peanut butter
8 tablespoons chocolate syrup
3 pancakes from breakfast tray

Directions
Set pancakes aside a moment and combine remaining ingredients: Mix well. Spread the mixture over the pancakes and enjoy your fine dining. This is also great with snack crackers. If no chocolate syrup is available, you can substitute with hot chocolate mix. Just make it as thick as syrup.

I would rather be a superb meteor, every atom of me in magnificent glow, than be a sleepy and permanent planet.
– Jack London

Peanut Butter Oatmeal

Ingredients
2 coffee mugs instant oatmeal (any flavor)
3/4 coffee mug hot water
1 teaspoon sweetener or 2 tablespoons sugar
1/2 coffee mug instant milk
3 tablespoons peanut butter
1 Butterfinger candy bar

Directions
Using a large spread bowl, combine oatmeal, instant milk, and hot water. Mix well and cover the bowl for 3-5 minutes. Now add the sweetener (or sugar) and peanut butter. Crush the candy bar and stir into the bowl. Quick, fast, and good!

*When one door closes, another opens;
but we often look so long and so regretfully upon the closed door
that we do not see the one that has opened for us.
– Alexander Graham Bell*

Helpful Cooking Tips

To hull strawberries, use a sturdy plastic straw. Push it up through the bottom of the strawberry and through the top. It does a great job quickly and neatly. The berries look excellent if you want to leave them whole.

For a different flavor and less fat, use chicken stock instead of butter or milk when whipping up mashed potatoes.

Use greased muffin tins as molds when baking stuffed peppers.

Making noodles is easy by adding an egg to a package of pie crust mix. Mix, roll out, cut, and let dry.

Keep a small plastic bag inside your can of vegetable shortening. When it comes time to grease a pan, just slip your hand in the bag, scoop out what you need, and spread it on the pan.

Use a 1 1/2-inch natural bristle paintbrush dipped in melted margarine or oil to grease muffin tins, cookie sheets, or cake and bread pans. It's much faster than using a skimpy pastry brush.

To slice meat into thin strips, as for Chinese dishes, partially freeze it, and it will slice easily.

A roast with the bone in will cook faster than a boneless roast – the bone carries the heat to the inside of the roast quicker.

To hasten the cooking of foods in a double boiler, add salt to the water in the outer boiler.

No "curly" bacon for breakfast when you dip it into cold water before frying.

A dampened paper towel or terry cloth brushed downward on a cob of corn will remove every strand of corn silk.

When working with dough, don't flour your hands; coat them with olive oil to prevent sticking.

Section 12:
Ad-Seg Delights

Ad-Seg Goo-Losh

Ingredients
1 (1.3 oz.) jalapeno pepper (singles)
1 (8 oz.) serving chili mac from tray
3 tablespoons squeeze cheese
1 (4 oz.) serving green beans from tray
1 (4 oz.) serving carrots from tray
2 tablespoons hot sauce
Slightly less than 1/4 coffee mug water
4 slices bread
pinch black pepper and salt

Directions
Dice jalapeno pepper into small pieces. Set bread aside. In a large chip bag, combine all remaining ingredients and mix well. Double bag and heat in a hot pot for 2 hours. If butter is available, butter bread and enjoy it with this meal.

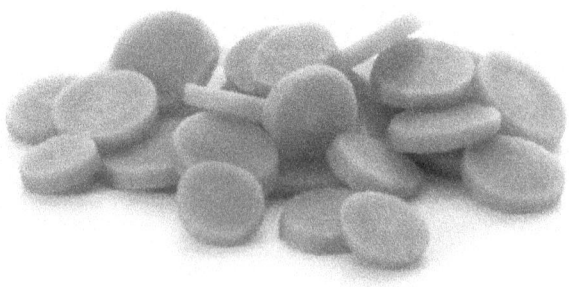

We are here to laugh at the odds and live our lives so well that death will tremble to take us.
– Charles Bukowski

Cheesy Chicken & Rice

Ingredients

1 chicken quarter or 2 chicken patties from tray
1 (1.3 oz.) jalapeno pepper (single)
1 package chicken Ramen seasoning
1/4 (8 oz.) bag instant white rice
1/2 teaspoon garlic powder
1 teaspoon onion powder
1/2 coffee mug hot water
1/4 (16 oz.) bottle squeeze cheese
2 tablespoons salsa

Directions

Shred chicken quarter or dice chicken patties. Dice jalapeno pepper. Set cheese and salsa aside. Combine remaining ingredients in a large chip bag and mix well. Double bag and heat in a hot pot for 2 hours. Stir occasionally. Add a little water if needed to keep moist. Once cooked, pour the mixture into a spread bowl and top with cheese and salsa.

It's a shallow life that doesn't give a person a few scars.
– Garrison Keillor

Troy Traylor

Chili Con Corn

Ingredients
2 (1.3 oz.) jalapeno peppers (singles)
1 (4 oz.) serving corn from tray
1 (4 oz.) serving green beans from tray
2 (11.25 oz.) packages chili with beans
1 coffee mug instant white rice
3 pieces corn bread
4 tablespoons instant milk
3 tablespoons squeeze cheese
2 coffee mugs hot water

Directions
Dice jalapeno peppers into small pieces. Set corn bread aside. In a large, clean chip bag, combine remaining ingredients and mix well. Double bag and heat in a hot pot for 3 hours. Stir occasionally. Once cooked, pour the mixture into a spread bowl. Crumble up corn bread, add to the bowl, and mix again. If you want to add a little spice, add a shot of your favorite hot sauce.

Regrets are as personal as fingerprints.
– Margaret Culkin Banning

Fine Dining Prison Cookbook 2

Good Ole Cabbage & Ham

Ingredients
4 (3 oz.) packages Spam or ham
4 (4 oz.) servings cabbage from tray

Directions
Dice Spam (or ham) into medium-sized cubes. In a large chip bag, combine all ingredients and mix well. If you have no juice from cabbage, just add 1/3 of a coffee mug of hot water. Double bag and heat in a hot pot for 4 hours. Once cooked, place all in a spread bowl and eat up. If you can get a shot of vinegar, drizzle it over the top of this dish.

*Genius might be the ability
to say a profound thing in a simple way.
– Charles Bukowski*

Troy Traylor

Greens & Ham

Ingredients
2 (3 oz.) packages Spam
1 tablespoon onion flakes
1 heaping serving spinach or greens from tray
1/4 coffee mug hot water
pinch salt and black pepper

Directions
Dice Spam into small cubes. Using a large clean chip bag, combine all ingredients, mix well, double bag, and heat in a hot pot for 2 hours. Drain juices and fill bowl with mixture. Buttered bread or saltines can really top off this meal.

*The most common way people give up their power
is by thinking they don't have any.
– Alice Wlaker, Pulitzer Prize for Fiction recipient*

Hungry Man Hobo

Ingredients
1 (3 oz.) beef Ramen noodles
1/2 teaspoon garlic powder
1 teaspoon onion powder
1 teaspoon onion flakes
1 coffee mug hot water
1 coffee mug ground beef from tray
1 (4 oz.) serving carrots from tray
1 (4 oz.) serving green beans from tray
Habanero sauce to taste
Good shot squeeze cheese
4 slices bread
butter if available

Directions
Set bread aside and combine all ingredients in a large chip bag. Mix well. Double bag and heat in a hot pot for 1 hour. Once cooked, pour the mixture into a spread bowl. Butter bread if available and eat up. You can substitute almost any of the vegetables.

Sadness is a wall between two gardens.
– Kahlil Gibran

Pork & Sauerkraut

Ingredients
3 pork chops from tray
1 (3 oz.) package Spam
1/3 coffee mug hot water
1/2 (2.75 oz.) bag pork skins
2 (4 oz.) serving sauerkraut from tray

Directions
Dice pork chops and Spam. Lightly crush pork skins. Using a large chip bag, combine all ingredients and mix well. Double bag and heat in a hot pot for 3 hours. You can add a sprinkle of black pepper if you desire. Pour the mixture into a spread bowl to serve. I really love this meal.

*The first to apologize is the bravest.
The first to forget is the happiest.
– Unknown*

Seg-Soft Tacos

Ingredients
2 (1.3 oz.) jalapeno peppers (singles)
4 flour tortillas
4 tablespoons squeeze cheese
1 (8 oz.) serving ground beef from tray
1 (4 oz.) serving corn from tray
1 package beef or chili Ramen seasoning
1 (2 oz.) package cream cheese
8 tablespoons salsa

Directions
Dice the jalapeno peppers into small pieces. Coat flour tortillas with squeeze cheese. Set salsa aside. In a spread bowl, combine the meat, corn, Ramen seasoning, cream cheese, and pepper pieces. Mix well. Spoon mixture onto flour tortillas and fold in half. Place these tacos in a rice bag and heat in a hot pot for 2 hours. Once they are cooked, place the tacos in your spread bowl and top with the salsa.

Nothing makes us so lonely as our secrets.
– Paul Tornier

Troy Traylor

Soup Salad

Ingredients
1 (3 oz.) shrimp Ramen noodles
1 (1.3 oz.) jalapeno pepper (single)
3 tablespoons squeeze cheese
1 tablespoon salad dressing
1 teaspoon black pepper
1 teaspoon onion powder
1 1/4 coffee mugs hot water
1/4 (9 oz.) pickle (any flavor)
1 (4 oz.) serving mixed vegetables from tray
10 tablespoons pickle juice (contents 1 package)
1/2 teaspoon garlic powder
1 (2 oz.) package ranch dressing

Directions
This is a cold dish. Crush Ramen and in a spread bowl, combine Ramen, seasoning, and hot water. Cover bowl tightly and steep for 5 minutes. While waiting, dice jalapeno pepper and pickle into small pieces. Once Ramen has cooked, drain any remaining water and rinse noodles in cold water. Set ranch dressing aside for a moment. Combine the remaining ingredients with the Ramen and mix well. Pour ranch dressing over the top. A Ramen has never been so good!

Imagination is more important than knowledge, for knowledge is limited while imagination embraces the world.
– Albert Einstein

Section 13:
Icings

Peanut Butter Cream

You can make this icing in one of two ways. The first way is to separate the cream from the peanut butter cream cookies. Set cookies aside. Combine cream with 4 heaping tablespoons of coffee creamer or instant milk. If you use the instant milk, you should add 2 teaspoons of sweetener or 4 tablespoons of sugar and add 3 tablespoons of hot water into an insert cup. Do not stir just yet. Heat the insert cup in a hot pot for 30 minutes, and then whip until creamy. Place back in the hot pot for an additional 30 minutes. You want this thick, like free-world icing. You may need to add a drop or two of water. Once cooked, whip well and pour over your dessert. Even out and let it sit for 1 hour. This will lock up then.

The second way is to separate cream from Duplex or vanilla cream cookies and combine the cream with ½ tablespoon peanut butter and 3 tablespoons of hot water in your insert cup. Again, do not stir yet; place your insert in a hot pot for 30 minutes, and then whip well. Place back in the hot pot for an additional 30 minutes. It will have a yellowish liquid floating on top. Pour this off and then spread the icing over your dessert. Let this set up for an hour.

Strawberry or Raspberry Cream

There are two ways to make this icing as well, and both generally follow the same directions as above. For the first, use strawberry cream cookies and follow the instructions for the first way to make peanut butter cream.

The second way is to use Duplex or vanilla cream cookies along with 1 heaping tablespoon of strawberry or raspberry Kool-Aid and follow the instructions for the second way to make peanut butter icing.

Vanilla Cream

Separate cream from Duplex or vanilla cream cookies. Place cream in an insert cup with 1 tablespoon of water. Do not stir just yet. Heat the insert cup in a hot pot for 30 minutes. Whip well and place back in the hot pot for an additional 30 minutes. Pour off yellowish liquid, whip, and pour over dessert.

Cinnamon, Butterscotch & Lemon Icing

All three of these icings can be created by using 10 pieces of the various flavored candies (crushed and melted). Cinnamon comes from using fireball candies; Lemon flavor will come from lemon candies or lemon electrolyte (1 teaspoon) or lemon Kool-Aid (2 tablespoons), and butterscotch comes from using butterscotch candies.

*All flavors of Kool-Aid can be used when making icings. Just add 1 tablespoon Kool-Aid with cream from a Duplex, vanilla cream cookie, along with 1 tablespoon water. Use your insert cup to combine all the ingredients and heat in the hot pot for 30 minutes before you whip. Whip well and place back in the hot pot for an additional 30 minutes. Pour off the yellowish liquid and pour it over your dessert.

- Yellowish liquid is sugar and oils separating from the cream.
- No matter what flavor you use, you will love the sweet taste. Don't be afraid to experiment.
- You can also use cream cheese and sugar to make your homemade icing. Again, add whatever flavor you want to create your desired taste.

Helpful Cooking Tips

Poke a hole in the middle of the hamburger patties while shaping them. The burgers will cook faster, and the holes will disappear when done.

A high-quality hard-boiled egg slicer makes easy work of slicing mushrooms for sauces or salads; it will also slice strawberries and peeled kiwi fruits perfectly.

To make deviled eggs with no mess, put the egg yolks from hard-boiled eggs in a plastic sandwich bag. Add remaining ingredients, close the bag, and mix. When finished, cut the small tip off the corner of the bag and squeeze into the hollowed egg white, then simply throw away the bag.

Fresh ginger will last longer if stored in a pot of sand.

Dried-out coconut can be revitalized by sprinkling with milk and letting it stand for about ten minutes.

Don't have a roasting pan? Make a rack out of vegetables like celery, carrots, and onions, and place your chicken, turkey, or roast on top. The excess fat drips away from the meat, and your pan drippings will be more flavorful.

Rescue stale or soggy chips and crackers: Preheat the oven to 300° F. Spread the chips or crackers in a single layer on a baking sheet and bake for about 5 minutes. Allow to cool, then seal in a plastic bag or container.

The best way to store fresh celery is to wrap it in aluminum foil and put it in the refrigerator. It will keep for weeks.

To make your own cornmeal mix: combine 1 cup cornmeal, 1 cup all-purpose flour, 1/2 teaspoon salt, and 4 teaspoons baking powder. You can store it in a tightly covered container for up to 6 months.

Section 14:
Pie Crusts & Pies

Troy Traylor

Chocolate Crust

Ingredients
1 (12 oz.) Coca Cola
2 coffee mugs hot chocolate mix
1 tablespoon peanut butter
1 coffee mug instant milk
3/4 coffee mug regular instant oatmeal

Directions
In a large spread bowl, combine hot chocolate mix, instant milk, peanut butter, oatmeal, and 4 tablespoons Coca Cola. Mix well with a spoon at first, and then knead into a pliable dough. You want this moist enough so that it sticks together. You may need to add a tablespoon more Coca Cola as you knead, but do not make it too moist. Once kneaded, flatten the dough out on the bottom of spread bowl. Starting in the center, using your knuckles, press down firmly, working your way around the bowl towards the outside. Dough will begin to climb the sides of the bowl. Work this into your crust. Sides of the crust should be halfway to 3/4 of the way up the sides of the bowl. Smooth out once done and place the bowl under a fan to dry for 4 hours. This crust takes a little longer to dry than others. While waiting, grab all your favorite ingredients and make your filling. See the icing for your topping.

Never confuse a single defeat with a final defeat.
– F. Scott Fitzgerald

Sticky Sweet Pie Crust

Ingredients
16 vanilla or peanut butter cream cookies
3 tablespoons honey
1 tablespoon peanut butter
5 tablespoons hot water
3/4 coffee mug maple brown sugar oatmeal

Directions

Separate the cream from the cookies and set the cream aside. Crush cookies as fine as possible. In a large spread bowl combine all ingredients except cream from cookies. Knead into pliable dough, just moist enough to stick together. Once kneaded, flatten the mixture out on the bottom of the spread bowl. Starting in the center, using your knuckles, press down firmly as you work your way around the bowl, towards the outside. Dough will begin to climb the sides. Work this into your pie crust. You want the crust about 3/4 the way up the sides of the bowl. Smooth out once done. Place the bowl under a fan to dry for 2-3 hours. If your unit has no honey, you can substitute it with syrup from a breakfast tray. While the crust dries, grab all your favorite ingredients and make your filling. Make icing out of cream from cookies.

Abundance is not something we acquire.
It is something we tune into.
– Dr. Wayne Dyer

Troy Traylor

Butter-Chocolate Cream Pie

Ingredients
1 (16 oz.) package vanilla cream cookies
1 coffee mug hot chocolate mix
3/4 coffee mug instant milk
1 tablespoon peanut butter
1 (1 oz.) Chick-O-Stick
1 (12 oz.) Sprite
1/4 coffee mug regular instant oatmeal
1 tsp. lemon lime electrolyte or 2 tbsps. Kool-Aid
1 package M&M's

Directions
Separate the cream from the cookies and set the cream aside. Crush cookies into a fine powder and place in a large spread bowl. Add 4 1/2 tablespoons Sprite to the bowl and knead into a pliable dough. You may need to add a half tablespoon more as you knead. You only want the dough moist enough to stick together. Flatten the dough out evenly on the bottom of a spread bowl. Beginning in the center, using your knuckles, press down firmly, working your way to the outside. Dough will begin to climb the sides. Work this into your pie crust and smooth out once done. Set this bowl under a fan for 2-3 hours. While waiting, using a separate spread bowl, combine hot chocolate mix, oatmeal, and 4 tablespoons Sprite. Knead this and flatten it out in your bowl. Set the pie crust to dry. Once dry, use your ID to run around inside the bowl with hot chocolate mix. Turn the bowl upside down to remove. Set this inside your pie crust and press firmly. Now, using the same bowl, combine instant milk, electrolyte (or Kool-Aid), and 6 tablespoons Sprite. Use two spoons and whip until smooth, creamy, and thick. Add peanut butter and M&Ms to the mixture and whip again. Pour the mixture into the pie crust and smooth out. Set the bowl under a fan to dry for 1-2 hours. Crush Chick-O-Stick and top off during dry time. You will crave more. Save the cream from cookies for another dessert.

Chocolate Almond Cherry Pie

Ingredients
1 (16 oz.) package vanilla cream cookies
2 Snickers bars
1/2 coffee mug instant milk
1/4 coffee mug hot water
8 tablespoons French vanilla cappuccino
2 (4 oz.) cherry pies

Directions
This pie will take a little time, but it is worth the wait. Separate the cream from the cookies and set the cream aside. Crush cookies into a fine powder and place in a large spread bowl. Add 4 1/2 tablespoons hot water to the bowl and knead into a pliable dough. You want this just moist enough, so it sticks together. Once kneaded, flatten out the dough evenly into the bottom of the spread bowl. Use your knuckles and press down on the dough to create a 1-inch lip around the bowl. Place the bowl under a fan to dry for 2 hours. One hour before it is dry, dice a Snickers bar. Using a rice bag, combine cappuccino, instant milk, Snickers bar pieces, and 3 tablespoons hot water. Heat this bag in a hot pot for the remaining hour. Once the crust is dry, remove the bag from the hot pot, whip, and pour into the crust. Allow this to sit under a fan for 2-3 hours. While waiting, remove filling from cherry pies and place filling in an insert cup with cream from cookies and 1 tablespoon hot water. Fully melt filling and cream in a hot pot insert. Once the crust is dry, pour the cream mixture over the pie. Again, place under a fan to dry for 2 more hours before you cut and serve.

From error to error one discovers the entire truth.
– Sigmund Freud

Troy Traylor

Chocolate Malt Ball Pie

Ingredients
1 (16 oz.) package Duplex cookies
1 1/2 coffee mugs instant milk
1/4 (16 oz.) bottle chocolate syrup
4 1/2 tablespoons hot water
6 tablespoons French vanilla cappuccino
14 malt balls

Directions
Separate the cream from the cookies and set the cream aside. Crush cookies into a fine powder and place all in a large spread bowl. Add hot water to this and knead into pliable dough, just moist enough so it sticks together. Flatten the dough out into the bottom of the bowl. Starting in the center, using your knuckles, press down firmly, working your way towards the outside. Dough will begin to climb the sides. Work this into your pie crust. Smooth out once done. Place this bowl under a fan to dry for 2 hours. Once dry, in a separate bowl, combine instant milk, cappuccino, and chocolate syrup, and then whip until smooth, creamy, and very thick. Once whipped, add malt balls and whip again. Pour the mixture into the pie crust and smooth out. Place the bowl back under a fan to dry for 2 more hours before you cut. Save the cream from cookies for another recipe.

Everyone needs to be valued.
Everyone has the potential to give something back.
— Princess Diana

Cinnamon Twist Crunch

Ingredients
1 (16 oz.) package vanilla cream cookies
1/2 coffee mug hot water
1 (3 oz.) Ramen noodles (any flavor)
1/2 coffee mug apple cinnamon oatmeal
1/4 coffee mug cinnamon and spice oatmeal
3 oatmeal cream pies
1/2 (2 oz.) package salted peanuts
1 coffee mug hot chocolate mix
1 (2 oz.) package cream cheese
5 butterscotch candies

Directions
You will need 3 large spread bowls. Separate the cream from the cookies and set the cream and 14 cookie halves aside. Crush the remaining cookies into a fine powder and put them in a large spread bowl. Add 3 tablespoons of hot water to this and knead into a pliable dough. Flatten out the mixture in the bottom of spread bowl and starting in the center, using your knuckles, press down firmly, working towards the outside of the bowl. Dough will begin to climb the sides of the bowl. Work this into a crust and smooth out once done. Place the bowl  under a fan for 2 hours. While waiting, crush Ramen into a fine powder. (This takes some work. I use a cheese bottle and crush 1/3 at a time in its bag.) Place this in bowl #2, add 14 cookie halves, oatmeal, oatmeal cream pies, peanuts, and 8 tablespoons hot water. Mix this thoroughly and evenly distribute

it in the bowl. Sit this with the crust to dry. In bowl #3, mix the hot chocolate mix with 3 tablespoons of hot water. Set this bowl aside until everything is dry. In the meantime, combine the cream from the cookies with the cream cheese in an instant cup. Heat the insert in a hot pot, stirring occasionally. Crush the butterscotch candies. Once all is dry, take the hot chocolate mixture and place it inside the pie crust. Press around firmly so the bottom of the crust is covered. Now, remove the oatmeal mixture and top this. Again, press firmly and even out. Remove insert from hot pot, whip well, and pour over pie. Decorate with butterscotch candies. Place the bowl back under a fan for 2 more hours before you cut it.

It is only too easy to compel a sensitive human being to feel guilty about anything.
– Morton Irving Seiden

Double Fudge Deluxe

Ingredients
1 (16 oz.) package peanut butter cream cookies
25 butterscotch candies
1/2 coffee mug hot water
1 (3 oz.) Ramen noodles (any flavor)
1 1/2 coffee mugs hot chocolate mix
1 (2 oz.) package cream cheese
1/2 (2 oz.) package salted peanuts

Directions
Crush candies and place in an insert with 2 tablespoons of hot water. Heat the insert in a hot pot until fully melted. Crush Ramen into a fine powder. (I use a full cheese bottle and crush 1/3 at a time in its bag.) In a large spread bowl, combine Ramen powder, melted candies, and hot chocolate mix. Mix well. Separate the cream from the cookies. Crush 14 of the cookie halves and add to the bowl. Mix again. Evenly flatten this mixture into the bottom of the bowl. Set the bowl under a fan for about 4 hours. While waiting, crush the rest of the cookies and place them in a separate spread bowl with 3 1/2 tablespoons of hot water. Knead into pliable dough. Even out the spread bowl and starting in the center, using your knuckles, press down firmly, working your way around the bowl, towards the outside. Dough will begin to climb the sides, forming your crust. Place the bowl with the filling to dry. Once filling is dry, run ID around bowl to loosen and turn bowl upside down to remove. Place filling inside the crust and press firmly. Set aside. In an insert cup, combine the cream from the cookies and the cream cheese. Whip and heat in a hot pot for 30 minutes. Whip occasionally. Pour this over the pie and decorate with peanuts. Allow to dry 1 hour before you cut and serve.

The scariest moment is always just before you start.
– Stephen King

Troy Traylor

End of the Road

Ingredients
1 (16 oz.) package cream cookies (any flavor)
1/2 coffee mug hot water
2 (1 oz.) Chick-O-Sticks
20 butterscotch candies
1 (3 oz.) Ramen noodles (any flavor)
1/2 coffee mug cinnamon & spice oatmeal
1 heaping tablespoon peanut butter
2 teaspoons sweetener or 4 tablespoons sugar
1 (4 oz.) serving mixed fruit from tray

Directions
Separate the cream from the cookies and set the cream aside with 14 cookie halves. In a large, spread bowl, crush the remaining cookies into a fine powder. Add 3 tablespoons of hot water and knead into the dough. Flatten out into the bottom of the bowl and, starting in the center, using your knuckles, press down firmly, working your way around the bowl, towards the outside. Dough will begin to climb the sides. Work this into your pie crust and smooth out when done. Place the bowl under a fan to dry for 2 hours. Now crush Chick-O-Sticks, butterscotch, and Ramen. Best to crush 1/3 Ramen at a time in its bag. The cheese bottle works best. In a separate spread bowl, combine remaining ingredients with 8 tablespoons hot water and mix thoroughly, even out in the bowl, and set aside with the crust. In an insert cup, combine the cream from the cookies with 1 tablespoon of hot water. Heat insert in a hot pot, stirring occasionally. Once dry, remove the oatmeal mixture from its bowl and put it in the pie crust. Even out and press firmly. Remove insert from hot pot, whip, and pour over pie. Smooth out and set back under a fan for 2 hours before you cut.

Fine Dining Prison Cookbook 2

Oatmeal Apple Pie

Ingredients
1 (16 oz.) package Duplex cookies
1 (4 oz.) apple pie
1 large cinnamon roll
1 teaspoon sweetener or 2 tablespoons sugar
1/3 coffee mug hot water
3/4 coffee mug apple cinnamon, and spice oatmeal
1 (3 oz.) Ramen noodles (any flavor)

Directions
Separate the cream from the cookies and set the cream aside. Crush all cookies into a fine powder and place in a large spread bowl. Add 4 1/2 tablespoons hot water to the bowl and knead into a pliable dough. Flatten out the dough at the bottom of the bowl and, starting in the center, using your knuckles, press down firmly, working your way around the bowl, towards the outside. Dough will begin to climb the sides. Work this into your pie crust and smooth out once done. Place the bowl under a fan to dry for 2 hours. Remove the apple filling from the pie and put it in an insert cup with the cream from the cookies and 1 tablespoon of hot water. Heat in a hot pot while the crust dries, stirring occasionally. In a separate spread bowl combine all the oatmeal. Dice the cinnamon roll and add to the bowl. Carefully crush Ramen into a fine powder. It is best to crush 1/3 at a time in its bag using a full cheese bottle. Now add the Ramen, sweetener (or sugar), and 6 tablespoons of hot water to the bowl and thoroughly mix. Spread the mixture evenly in a bowl and place it next to the crust to dry. Once the crust is dry, remove the oatmeal mixture from its bowl and set it inside the crust. Press down firmly. Remove insert from hot pot, whip, and pour over top of pie. Even out. Place the bowl back under the fan for 2 hours before you cut.

Troy Traylor

Oatmeal Cream Pie

Ingredients
1 (16 oz.) package Duplex cream cookies
1/3 coffee mug hot water
1 box (10 packages) instant oatmeal (variety flavors)
4 (2 oz.) packages cream cheese
4 oatmeal cream pies
1 1/2 tablespoons peanut butter
1 package M&Ms

Directions
Separate the cream from the cookies and set the cream aside. Crush all cookies into a fine powder and place in a large spread bowl. Add 4 1/2 tablespoons hot water to this and knead into a pliable dough. Flatten out the dough into the bottom of the bowl and, starting in the center, using your knuckles, press down firmly, working your way around the bowl, towards the outside. Dough will begin to climb the sides of the bowl. Work this into your crust and smooth out once done. Place the bowl under a fan to dry for 2 hours. While waiting, in a separate spread bowl combine all oatmeal, cream cheese, oatmeal cream pies, peanut butter, and all but 1 tablespoon hot water. Mix this thoroughly and flatten out in a bowl. Set this bowl with the crust until the crust is ready. Now combine the cream from the cookies and 1 tablespoon of hot water in an instant cup and heat in a hot pot. Whip occasionally. Once the crust is dry, run the ID card around the bowl with the oatmeal mixture, turn upside down, and remove. Place this inside the pie crust and press firmly. Remove insert from hot pot, whip, and pour over pie. Even out and cool under a fan for 1 hour before you cut.

Every next level of your life will demand a different you.
– Unknown

One Sweet Chocolate Pie

Ingredients
1 (16 oz.) package Duplex cream cookies
1 coffee mug hot chocolate mix
3 oatmeal cream pies
2 (1 oz.) Chick-O-Sticks
1/3 coffee mug hot water
1/4 (18 oz.) jar peanut butter
1 (3 oz.) Ramen noodles (any flavor)
4 tablespoons French vanilla cappuccino

Directions

Separate the cream from the cookies and set the cream aside. Also, set aside 16 vanilla halves from these cookies. Crush the remaining cookies into a fine powder and place in a large spread bowl. Add 3 1/2 tablespoons hot water to this and knead into a pliable dough. (You may need to add as much as 1/2 tablespoon of water as you knead, but you only want this moist enough to stick together.) Flatten out the dough into the bottom of the bowl. Starting in the center, press down firmly, working your way around the bowl towards the outside. Dough will begin to climb the sides of the bowl. Work this into your pie crust and smooth when done. Place the bowl under a fan to dry for 2-3 hours. In a separate bowl, combine hot chocolate mix, peanut butter, oatmeal cream pies, and remaining cookie halves. Crush Ramen into a powder. This takes work, and it's best to do a 1/3 at a time in the bag. Add this powder to a bowl with about 1/4 coffee mug of hot water and knead well. Flatten out the mixture into the bottom of the bowl and set it under a fan to dry with the crust. Crush the Chick-O-Sticks and inside an insert cup, combine

Chick-O-Sticks, cream from cookies, cappuccino, and 1 1/2 tablespoons hot water. Heat insert cup in a hot pot, stirring occasionally. Make sure everything is melted by heating for 1 hour. When all is ready, use your ID to run around the edges of a bowl of hot chocolate mixture. Turn the bowl upside down and carefully remove the mixture and place it inside the pie crust. Press down firmly. Remove insert from hot pot, whip, and pour over pie. Even out the icing and set aside to cool for 1 hour. Cut and serve.

> *Guilt not only doesn't decrease our negative behaviors, it guarantees their repetition.*
> *– Allen Nagy*

Raisin Nut Delight

Ingredients
1 (16 oz.) package vanilla cream or Duplex cream cookies
1/2 coffee mug hot water
1 tablespoon coffee
2 heaping tablespoons hot chocolate mix
1 (3 oz.) Ramen noodles (any flavor)
1/2 coffee mug raisin and spice oatmeal
1/4 coffee mug regular oatmeal
1/2 (2 oz.) package salted peanuts
2 teaspoons sweetener or 4 tablespoons sugar
3 oatmeal cream pies
1 (4 oz.) serving raisins from tray
1 package nutty bars
20 pieces butterscotch candies

Directions
Separate the cream from the cookies and set the cream aside. Put 14 cookie halves aside and crush the rest as fine as possible. Place crushed cookies in a large spread bowl. Fill a coffee mug halfway with hot water, add coffee and hot chocolate mix to the cup, and mix well. Add 3 1/2 tablespoons coffee mixture to the bowl and knead into a pliable dough. Flatten the dough out into the bottom of the bowl and, starting in the center, using your knuckles, press down firmly, working your way towards the outside of the bowl. Dough will begin to climb the sides. Work this into your pie crust and smooth out once done. Place the bowl under a fan for 2 hours. While waiting, using a full cheese bottle, crush Ramen into a fine powder, about a 1/3 at a time, in its bag. Pour this powder into a separate spread bowl. Add 9 tablespoons of coffee mixture to the bowl and cover for 3 minutes. Break up 14 cookie halves into quarters and add to the bowl. Crush nutty bars and butterscotch candies. Add all remaining ingredients to the bowl with 4 tablespoons of coffee

mixture. Knead this and flatten it out on the bottom of a spread bowl. Set the bowl with the crust until it is dry. Put the cream from the cookies in an insert cup with 1 tablespoon of coffee mixture and heat the insert in a hot pot until fully melted. Once all is ready, use your ID card to run around the oatmeal mixture. Turn the bowl upside down to remove the mixture and put it in the pie crust, and press firmly. Remove cream from hot pot, whip well, and pour over pie. Place the bowl back under a fan for 2 more hours.

It is hard to be happier than other people because we always believe others to be happier than they really are.
– Montesquieu

Reese's Pieces Pie

Ingredients
1 (16 oz.) package vanilla cream cookies
1/3 coffee mug hot water
1 coffee mug hot chocolate mix
2 heaping tablespoons peanut butter
1 (3 oz.) Ramen noodles (any flavor)
2 (1 oz.) Chick-O-Sticks
1 brick graham crackers
1 teaspoon sweetener or 2 tablespoons sugar
1/2 coffee mug instant maple brown sugar oatmeal

Directions
You will need 3 large spread bowls. Separate the cream from the cookies and set the cream aside. Crush all cookies into a fine powder and place in a large spread bowl. Add 4 1/2 tablespoons hot water to the bowl and knead into a pliable dough. You only want the dough moist enough, so it all sticks together. You may need to add a half spoonful more of water as you knead. Flatten the mixture out into the bottom of the bowl and, starting in the center, using  your knuckles, press down firmly, working your way around the bowl, towards the outside. Dough will begin to climb the sides. Work this into a pie crust and smooth out. Place the bowl under a fan to dry for 2 hours. While waiting, grab 2 more spread bowls. In 1 bowl, combine hot chocolate mix, 1 tablespoon peanut butter, and 2 tablespoons hot water. Mix well and place

in an insert cup. Heat the insert in a hot pot for one hour while the crust dries. Stir occasionally. Use a full cheese bottle and crush Ramen into a super fine powder. This takes work. It's easiest to do 1/3 at a time in its bag. Now, crush Chick-O-Sticks and graham crackers, and remove the insert container from the hot pot. In the last bowl, combine remaining ingredients with 4 tablespoons hot water and mix well. Flatten this mixture out into the bowl and place the bowl with the pie crust. Now add the cream from the cookies and the peanut butter to the cup and stir well. Allow to heat for the remaining hour, stirring occasionally. Once the crust is dry, run your ID card around the bowl with the hot chocolate mixture in it to loosen the mixture. Turn the bowl upside down and carefully remove the mixture. Place this inside the pie crust, press down firmly, and even out. Remove the insert cup from the hot pot, whip, and pour over the pie. Even out and place under a fan for 2 more hours. Cut and serve.

Who looks outside, dreams, who looks inside, awakes.
– Carl Jung

Snicker Doodle Delight

Ingredients
1 1/2 (16 oz.) packages vanilla cream cookies
1/2 coffee mug hot water
3 Snickers bars
4 tablespoons hot chocolate mix
2 packages nutty bars
1 1/2 coffee mugs instant milk
2 (2 oz.) packages salted peanuts

Directions
Separate the cream from the cookies and set the cream aside. Crush all cookies into a fine powder and place all in a large spread bowl. Add 5 1/2 tablespoons hot water to this and knead into a pliable dough, just moist enough to stick together. (You may need to add another half to a whole tablespoon of water.) Flatten dough out into the bottom of your spread bowl and, starting in the center, press down firmly, working towards the outside. Dough will begin to climb the sides of the bowl. Work this into a pie crust and smooth out once done. Place the bowl under a fan to dry for 2 hours. While waiting, dice Snickers bars and crush nutty bars. Melt diced Snickers in a hot pot insert. Once melted, in a separate spread bowl, combine Snickers bars, hot chocolate mix, nutty bars, instant milk, and 5 tablespoons hot water. Use two spoons and whip until smooth and creamy. You want this mixture very thick, like pancake batter, with no lumps or clumps. Add a half tablespoon of water if you desire as you whip. Add peanuts, stir, and pour into the pie crust. Smooth filling out and place the bowl under a fan to dry for 2-3 hours before you cut. This is an 8-piece dream pie.

Change your thoughts, and you change your world.
– Norman Vincent Peale

Troy Traylor

Sweet Potato Pie

Ingredients
1 (16 oz.) package vanilla cream cookies
1 (3 oz.) Ramen noodles (any flavor)
1 (4 oz.) serving raisins from tray
1 (1 oz.) Chick-O-Stick
1/4 coffee mug hot water
1/2 coffee mug maple brown sugar oatmeal
2 (4 oz.) servings sweet potatoes from tray

Directions
Separate the cream from the cookies and set the cream aside with 14 cookie halves. Crush remaining cookies and put in a large spread bowl. Add 3 tablespoons of hot water to the bowl and knead into a pliable dough. Flatten out into the bottom of the bowl and, starting in the center, using your knuckles, press down firmly, working your way around the bowl, towards the outside. The dough will begin to climb the sides. Work this into your pie crust and smooth out. Place the bowl under a fan to dry for 2 hours. Using a full cheese bottle to crush Ramen in its bag, 1/3 at a time. Make sure this is a fine powder. In a separate spread bowl, combine Ramen, oatmeal, raisins, sweet potatoes, 14 cookie halves, and 6 tablespoons of hot water. Mix thoroughly and cover the bowl. In an insert cup, combine the cream from the cookies and 1 tablespoon of hot water. Heat this mixture in a hot pot, stirring occasionally. Crush Chick-O-Stick. Once the dough is dry, put the sweet potato mixture into the pie crust and even it out. Remove insert from hot pot, whip, and pour over pie. Smooth out and decorate with Chick-O-Stick. Place the bowl back under a fan for 2 more hours before you cut and serve. You must eat this within a few hours, so you may want to invite a few associates.

Our life is what our thoughts make it.
– Marcus Aurelius

Section 15:
Cakes

Troy Traylor

Baltimore's Magic Trick

Ingredients
1 banana fudge ice cream bar
1/2 coffee mug hot chocolate mix
1 (2 oz.) package trail mix
1 (16 oz.) package cream cookies (any flavor)
2 tablespoons hot water

Directions
Heat the ice cream in a cup until fully melted. Separate the cream from the cookies and set the cream aside. Crush cookies into a fine powder and place in a large spread bowl. Add hot chocolate mix, all but 1 tablespoon of melted ice cream, and hot water to the bowl and knead into a pliable dough. Once kneaded evenly, flatten the dough out into the bottom of the spread bowl. Set under a fan to dry for 2 hours. In an insert cup, combine the cream from the cookies and the remaining ice cream. Heat the insert in a hot pot while the cake dries, stirring occasionally. Once the dough is dry, remove the insert from the hot pot, whip well, and pour over the cake. Decorate with an energy mix, and place back under a fan for 1 1/2 more hours. Cut and serve. Watch it disappear like magic.

In a gentle way, you can shake the world.
– Mahatma Gandhi

Chocolate Coconut Cake

Ingredients
1 (16 oz.) package vanilla cream cookies
1/4 coffee mug hot water
1 coffee mug hot chocolate mix
1 (16 oz.) bag vanilla wafers
10 (1 oz.) Chick-O-Sticks

Directions
Separate the cream from the cookies and set the cream aside. Crush cookies, vanilla wafers, and Chick-O-Sticks as fine as possible. Split this crushed mixture equally between 2 large spread bowls. Add 6 tablespoons of water to each bowl and knead into a pliable dough. You may need to add as much as a half a tablespoon of water to each bowl as you knead. However, you don't want this dough too wet, just moist enough to stick together. Now, combine both pieces from each bowl and knead together. Place in a bowl under a fan to dry for 2 hours. While waiting, in an insert cup, combine hot chocolate mix, cream from cookies, and 2 tablespoons hot water. Whip and place in a hot pot until the cake is dry. Whip once more after 30 minutes. Once the dough is dry, remove the insert from the hot pot, whip, and pour over the cake. Place back under a fan for 2 hours before you cut. This is simply the best cake.

It is not the prisoners who need reformation,
it is the prisons.
– Oscar Wilde

Troy Traylor

Chocolate-Toffee Cake

Ingredients
1 (16 oz.) package Duplex cream cookies
9 1/2 tablespoons hot water
1 coffee mug hot chocolate mix
25 pieces butterscotch candies
6 tablespoons French vanilla cappuccino

Directions
Separate the cream from the cookies and set the cream aside. Crush all cookies into a fine powder and place in a spread bowl. Add 4 1/2 tablespoons hot water to the bowl and knead into a pliable dough. You only want the dough moist enough to stick together. Crush all candies into tiny pieces. Place these pieces into an insert cup. Add remaining hot water to insert cup and heat insert in a hot pot to melt candies. Flatten the dough out into the bottom of the spread bowl and place the bowl under a fan to dry for 2 hours. Once candies are melted, add cream from cookies, cappuccino, and hot chocolate mix to the insert cup and whip well. Place back in a hot pot until the dry time is up. Once the cake is dry, remove the insert from the hot pot, whip well, and pour the mixture over the cake. Even out the icing and place the cake back under a fan for 2 hours. This one is simply great!

There are no ugly loves nor handsome prisons.
– Benjamin Franklin

Convict Cake

Ingredients
1 (16 oz.) package vanilla cream cookies
1/4 (16 oz.) bottle chocolate syrup
1/4 (18 oz.) jar peanut butter
1/4 (12 oz.) bottle strawberry preserves
4 1/2 tablespoons hot water
3 tablespoons butter (optional)
2 large cinnamon rolls (any flavor)
1 package M&Ms

Directions
Separate the cream from the cookies and set the cream aside. Crush cookies into a fine powder and place in a large spread bowl. Add 4 1/2 tablespoons hot water to the bowl and knead into a pliable dough. You only want the dough moist enough to stick together. Split the dough in half. Flatten one half out in a large spread bowl and repeat the process in a separate bowl with the other half. Dry both bowls with the dough under a fan for 2 hours. In an insert cup, combine the cream from the cookies, the chocolate syrup, the butter, and 1 tablespoon of peanut butter. Heat the insert in a hot pot while the cake dries, stirring occasionally. Cut cinnamon rolls into good-sized pieces. Once the cake is dry, run your ID around one bowl, turn the bowl upside down, and remove the cake. Spread the rest of the peanut butter over the cake in the bowl. Cover with cut-up cinnamon rolls and strawberry preserves. Cover with the second piece of cake and press down firmly. Remove the insert cup from the hot pot, whip, and pour over the cake. Decorate with M&Ms and place under a fan to dry for 2 hours before you cut.

The secret of getting ahead is getting started.
– Mark Twain

Troy Traylor

Dream Bar Cake

Ingredients
2 (16 oz.) packs vanilla cream cookies
2 tsps. orange electrolyte or 4 tbsps. orange Kool-Aid
1/4 coffee mug hot water
1 (10.25 oz.) bag orange slices
1 (2 oz.) package cream cheese

Directions
Separate the cream from the cookies and set the cream aside. Crush all cookies into a fine powder and equally divide between 2 large spread bowls. In a cup, combine the electrolyte (or Kool-Aid) and hot water. Stir until all is dissolved. Add 4 tablespoons of electrolyte mix into each bowl and knead into pliable doughs. Add up to another half tablespoon as needed to knead. You do not want the dough too wet, only moist enough to stick together. Flatten the dough out into the bottom of the spread bowls and even out. Place bowls under a fan for 2 hours to dry. In an insert cup, combine the cream from the cookies and 1 tablespoon of the electrolyte mixture, and heat in a hot pot. Stir occasionally. Dice orange slices into small pieces. Once dried, turn one bowl upside down and remove the cake. (Run your ID around the bowl to loosen.) Spread cream cheese over the cake in the bowl and top with half the orange slices. Top this with a second piece of cake. Press down firmly. Remove cream from the hot pot, whip, and pour over the top of the cake. Decorate with the other half of the orange slices. Allow the cake to sit for 1 1/2 hours before you cut. This is a dream come true.

Two roads diverged in a wood, and I – I took the one less traveled by, and that has made all the difference.
– Robert Frost, Pulitzer Prize for Poetry recipient

Gravitational Bliss

Ingredients
2 (16 oz.) packages Duplex cream cookies
2 heaping tablespoons peanut butter
4 (.78 oz.) Rice Crispy treats
1/2 coffee mug hot chocolate mix
4 packages nutty bars
1 (8 oz.) bag Bud's Best Butterfinger cookies
1 package M&Ms (plain)
1/2 coffee mug hot water
2 Snickers bars
8 oatmeal cream pies
2 (1 oz.) Chick-O-Sticks

Directions
Separate the cream from the cookies and set the cream aside. Crush all cookies as fine as possible and equally divide into two large spread bowls. Add 4 1/2 tablespoons hot water to each bowl and knead into pliable dough – just moist enough to stick, but not too wet. Evenly flatten the dough out into the bottom of these bowls. Place bowls under a fan to dry for 2 hours. While these dry, combine cream from the cookies, 1 1/2 tablespoons peanut butter, and 1 tablespoon hot water in an insert cup. Heat the insert in a hot pot. Stir after 30 minutes. Cut up the Snickers bars and Rice Crispy treats. Use your ID cards to separate oatmeal cream pies. In a separate spread bowl, combine hot chocolate mix, the rest of the peanut butter, and 3 tablespoons hot water. Whip until smooth and creamy. Once the dough has dried, run your ID around one bowl of dough to loosen and turn the bowl upside down to remove. Layer cake in this order: a layer of peanut butter mixture, 1 crushed Chick-O-Stick, half the Snickers bars, 2 packages nutty bars, half the Rice Crispy treats, and 1/3 of Bud's best cookies. Use half the oatmeal cream pie to cap off. Press down firmly. Now repeat all steps

again. Place the other half of the cake on top and again press firmly. Remove the insert cup from the hot pot, whip well, and pour over the cake. Now decorate with the remaining Bud's best cookies and M&Ms. This is a special treat for you and a couple of close associates.

You have to expect things of yourself before you can do them.
– Michael Jordan

Mini Fruitcake

Ingredients
8 chocolate chip cookies or 8 oatmeal cookies
1/2 coffee mug apple cinnamon instant oatmeal
1 heaping tablespoon peanut butter
1 heaping tablespoon strawberry preserves
1 (2 oz.) package trail mix
6 tablespoons hot water

Directions
Crush the cookies into a fine powder and place in a large spread bowl. Add remaining ingredients and knead into dough, just moist enough to stick together. Shape into any shape you desire. Place on a cookie wrapper or set in a bowl. Allow this to dry for 4 hours. Heat up the coffee; you'll really enjoy this one.

*Ever tried. Ever failed. No matter.
Try again. Fail again. Fail better.
– Samuel Beckett*

Troy Traylor

Peanut Butter & Jelly Cake

Ingredients
2 (16 oz.) packages vanilla or Duplex cream cookies
10 1/2 tablespoons hot water
1 coffee mug hot chocolate mix
2 heaping tablespoons peanut butter
1/4 (12 oz.) bottle grape jelly
1 (2 oz.) package cream cheese
1/4 (10 oz.) bag sunflower seeds (optional)

Directions
Separate the cream from the cookies and set the cream aside. Crush all cookies into a fine powder and equally divide between two large spread bowls. Add 4 tablespoons of hot water to each bowl and knead into a pliable dough. You may need to add another half tablespoon as you knead; you want a moist but not wet dough. Evenly flatten the dough out into the bottom of the spread bowls and place the bowls under a fan to dry for 2 hours. In an insert cup, combine hot chocolate mix, cream from cookies, and 2 tablespoons hot water, stir well, and heat in a hot pot. Once the cake is dry, run the ID card around one bowl to loosen the dough. Turn the bowl upside down to remove. Spread peanut butter and jelly evenly over the cake in the bowl. Top with cream cheese and sprinkle on sunflower seeds. Top with the second piece of cake and press firmly. Remove the insert from the hot pot and whip well. Pour this over the cake and smooth out. Place the bowl back under a fan for 2 hours before you cut it to serve.

Happiness is a butterfly which, when pursued, is always beyond our grasp, but if you will sit down quietly, may alight upon you.
– Nathaniel Hawthorne

Simply a Chocolate Cake

Ingredients
1 (16 oz.) package vanilla cream cookies
7 1/2 tablespoons hot water
1 coffee mug hot chocolate mix
1 Hershey bar (plain)

Directions
Separate the cream from the cookies and set the cream aside. Crush cookies into a fine powder and place in a large spread bowl. Add hot chocolate mix with 6 1/2 tablespoons of hot water to the bowl and knead into a pliable dough. You want it just moist enough to stick together. Evenly flatten the dough out into the bottom of the spread bowl. Place the bowl under a fan to dry for 2 hours. Combine the cream from the cookies with 1 tablespoon hot water. Place the insert in a hot pot to heat while the cake dries. Once the cake is dry, remove the insert from the hot pot, whip well, and pour over the top of the cake. Use whatever is available, shave a Hershey bar, and decorate the cake. Place the bowl back under a fan for 2 hours before you cut to serve.

As long as we are persistent in our pursuit of our deepest destiny, we will continue to grow. We cannot choose the day or time when we will fully bloom. It happens in its own time.
– Denis Waitley

Troy Traylor

Spice-E-Cake

Ingredients
1 (16 oz.) package vanilla cream cookies
4 fireball candies
2 teaspoons sweetener or 2 tablespoons sugar
5 1/2 tablespoons hot water
1 (2 oz.) package cream cheese

Directions
Separate the cream from the cookies and set the cream aside. Crush cookies into a fine powder and place in a large spread bowl. Add 4 1/2 tablespoons hot water to the bowl and knead into a pliable dough. You do not want the dough too wet, only moist enough to stick together. Flatten the dough out into the bottom of the spread bowl and even it out. Place the bowl under a fan to dry for 2 hours. While waiting, crush fireballs into small pieces and put them in an insert cup. Add cream cheese, sweetener (or sugar), and 1 tablespoon hot water and stir well. Place the insert cup into the hot pot, and melt the ingredients. Stir occasionally. Once the dough is dry, remove the insert cup from the hot pot, whip, and pour over the cake. Now, place the bowl back under a fan to dry for an additional 2 hours. All you can say about this is, "Wow!"

You will become as small as your controlling desire;
as great as your dominant aspiration.
– James Allen

Sweet Snickers Cake

Ingredients
4 Snickers candy bars
1 (16 oz.) package vanilla cream cookies
1 (2 oz.) packages cream cheese
4 1/2 tablespoons hot water

Directions
Dice all Snickers bars into small pieces. In an insert cup, combine Snickers bars and cream cheese. Place the insert in a hot pot to fully melt. Separate the cream from the cookies and add the cream to the instant cup. Crush all cookies as fine as possible and place in a large spread bowl. Add the hot water to the bowl and knead into pliable dough. Evenly flatten the dough into the bottom of the spread bowl. Place the bowl under a fan to dry for 2 hours. Once dried, remove the insert from the hot pot, whip well, and pour over the cake. Smooth out and place back under a fan for 2 hours before you cut. You're going to love this one!

The strongest principle of growth lies in human choice.
– George Hiot

Sweet Strawberry Cake

Ingredients
1 (16 oz.) package vanilla cream cookies
1 (16 oz.) bag vanilla wafers
1 coffee mug instant strawberry oatmeal
1 (12 oz.) strawberry soda
2 tablespoons strawberry preserves

Directions
Separate the cream from the cookies and set the cream aside. Crush all cookies and wafers into a fine powder. In a clean, large chip bag, combine cookies, wafers, and instant oatmeal. Add 10 tablespoons of soda to the bag and knead into a pliable dough. You may need to add another tablespoon as you knead. You want the dough just moist enough, so it sticks together. Flatten out the dough in the bag and then cut the bag open. Place under a fan to dry for 2 hours. Combine the cream from the cookies and the strawberry preserves in an insert cup and whip. Heat the insert cup in a hot pot while the cake dries. Once the cake is ready, remove the insert cup from the hot pot, whip well, and pour over the cake. Smooth out the icing and place it under a fan for an additional 2 hours. Cut and serve. Awesome!

> *Exert your talents, and distinguish yourself, and don't think of retiring from the world until the world will be sorry that you retired.*
> – Samuel Johnson

Texas Mudd

Ingredients
1 (12 oz.) package chocolate chip cookies
3 tablespoons hot water
1 Snickers bar
1 Hershey bar plain
1 (8 oz.) bag chocolate-covered peanuts
1 (1 oz.) Chick-O-Stick
4 malt balls
1 large chocolate moon pie

Directions
Crush cookies into a fine powder. In a large spread bowl, combine cookies, chocolate-covered peanuts, and hot water. Knead the dough and split it in half. Flatten one piece out on the bottom of the spread bowl. Set the other piece aside. Crush a Chick-O-Stick and dice a Snickers bar. Crush malt balls and dice Hershey bars into small pieces. In an insert cup, combine all these ingredients and place in a hot pot to melt. Separate the moon pie marshmallow from the cookie part. Dice a marshmallow. When ingredients in the hot pot are melted, pour half of them on the dough in the bowl. Cover the layer with diced marshmallow. Pour the remaining ingredients over this. Flatten out the remaining dough and top the cake. Press down firmly. Allow to dry for 3 hours before you cut. What a delight this is.

*Although the world is full of suffering,
it is also full of the overcoming of it.
– Helen Keller*

Troy Traylor

The Real Deal Cake

Ingredients
1 (16 oz.) box oatmeal cream pies
1 (12 oz.) Sprite
1 (16 oz.) package vanilla cream cookies
2 (1 oz.) Chick-O-Sticks
2 (3 oz.) Ramen noodles (any flavor)
4 teaspoons sweetener or 8 tablespoons sugar
1/4 coffee mug hot water
2 packages nutty bars

Directions
You will need 1 empty toilet paper roll, 1 small trash bag, and 2 spread bowls. This recipe takes time and patience, but the results are incredible. Stand the toilet paper roll in the center of a bowl. Cut the trash bag to cover the toilet paper roll and the bowl, with about 2 inches left hanging over the edge of the bowl. Set the rest of the bag aside. Take 8 oatmeal cream pies and split them in half using your ID card. Use the pies to form the crust, pressing the halves cream side down. Start from the middle, working around the toilet paper roll and working outwards, do not leave any gaps. Set this bowl aside. Grab a full cheese bottle and crush Ramen into powder. It's best to do this 1/3 at a time in its bag. It takes some work. Add a sweetener to the powder. Put this powder in the second spread bowl and pour in the Sprite and about a 1/4 coffee mug of hot water. Stir and cover for 15 minutes. While waiting, separate the cream from the cookies and set the cream aside. Do not crush cookies. Crush the Chick-O-Sticks and nutty bars in their package. Grab your bowl that has the crust and add layers in it this way: 1/3 of the cookies, spread evenly; 1/3 Ramen paste; 1 Chick-O-Stick; and 1 package of nutty bars. Repeat this layering one more time and top with a final row of cookies and remaining Ramen paste. Now take 4 oatmeal cream pies and split them in half with your ID.

Cover the top of the cake. Some gaps are okay. Press down firmly. Cover the bowl with a piece of the remaining trash bag and set aside for 24 hours. After 24 hours, flip the bowl over to remove. Press down firmly one more time. Remove the plastic from the cake and the toilet paper roll. You can melt cream from cookies and drizzle all over the cake, or use it for another recipe. If you melt cream, allow it to dry for 1 hour before you cut. Without a doubt, this is the real deal!

The best rules to form a young man are to talk little, to hear much, to reflect alone upon what has passed in company, to distrust one's own opinions, and value others that deserve it.
– Sir William Temple

Troy Traylor

Too Die for Cake

Ingredients
1 (16 oz.) package Duplex cream cookies
1 (2 oz.) package salted peanuts
1 tsp. lemon lime electrolyte or 2 tbsps. lemon Kool-Aid
1 heaping handful raisins
5 1/2 tablespoons hot water
1/4 teaspoon coffee

Directions
Separate the cream from the cookies and set the cream aside. Crush cookies into a fine powder and place in a large spread bowl. Add peanuts, electrolyte (or Kool-Aid), raisins, and 4 1/2 tablespoons hot water to the bowl and knead into a dough substance. You only want this dough moist enough, so it sticks together. Place the bowl under a fan to dry for 2 hours. While waiting, combine the cream from cookies, 1 tablespoon of hot water, and coffee in an insert cup and whip. Heat the insert cup in a hot pot. Whip occasionally. Once dry, remove the insert from the hot pot, whip, and pour over the cake. Even out and place back under a fan for 1 hour before you cut.

Fear less, hope more, eat less, chew more, whine less, breath more, talk less, say more, hate less, love more, and good things will be yours. – Swedish Proverb

Section 16:
Cheesecakes

Troy Traylor

Cheesecake #1

Ingredients
1 (13 oz.) box graham crackers
1 1/2 coffee mugs instant milk
3 (2 oz.) packages cream cheese
1 (12 oz.) Sprite
1 tsp. lemon lime electrolyte or 2 tbsps. Kool-Aid

Directions
Crush graham crackers into a fine powder and place all in a large spread bowl. Add 3 tablespoons of soda to the bowl and knead into a pliable dough. You only want dough moist enough to stick together. Flatten out the mixture in the bottom of the bowl, starting in the center, using your knuckles, press the dough down firmly, working your way around the bowl towards the outside. Dough will begin to climb the sides. Work this into your pie crust and smooth out once you're done. Place the bowl under a fan for 2 hours. Once the crust is dry, using another spread bowl, combine remaining ingredients with 5 tablespoons Sprite and whip with 2 spoons until smooth and creamy. You may need to add 1 more tablespoon of soda. You want this very thick, like pancake batter. Pour this mixture into the pie crust and even it out. Place the bowl back under a fan for 2 more hours before you cut and serve.

*The biggest adventure you will ever have
is to live the life of your dreams.
– Oprah*

Cheesecake #2

Ingredients
1 (16 oz.) package vanilla cream cookies
5 (2 oz.) packages cream cheese
4 teaspoons sweetener or 8 tablespoons sugar
5 1/2 tablespoons hot water
1 teaspoon lemon lime electrolyte or 2 tablespoons Kool-Aid
1 brick graham crackers

Directions
Separate the cream from the cookies and set the cream aside. Crush cookies into a fine powder and place in a large spread bowl. Add 4 1/2 tablespoons hot water to the bowl and knead into a pliable dough. Flatten dough out into the bottom of the bowl and starting in the center, press down firmly, working your way around the bowl, towards the outside. Dough will begin to climb the sides. Work this into your pie crust. Place the bowl under a fan for 2 hours. Once dry, set graham crackers aside and combine remaining ingredients in a large spread bowl. Whip until the cream from the cookies is smooth and creamy. Pour the mixture into the crust. Crush graham crackers and sprinkle over the top. Allow to sit for 4 hours before you cut and serve.

If we all did the things, we are capable of, we would astound ourselves.
– Thomas Edison

Big Red Apple Cheesecake

Ingredients
1 (13 oz.) box graham crackers
1 1/2 coffee mugs instant milk
2 (2 oz.) packages cream cheese
1 (12 oz.) Big Red soda
1 tsp. lemon lime electrolyte or 2 tbsps. Kool-Aid
3/4 coffee mug apple cinnamon instant oatmeal

Directions
Crush graham crackers in a large spread bowl. Add 3 tablespoons of soda to the bowl and knead into a pliable dough. Be careful if you need to add more soda, you only want this moist enough to stick together. Flatten out the mixture in the bottom of the bowl and, starting in the center, using your knuckles, press down firmly, working your way around the bowl, towards the outside. Dough will begin to climb the sides. Work this into your pie crust and smooth out once you're done. Place the bowl under a fan to dry for 2 hours. Once the crust is dry, using a separate bowl, combine instant milk, electrolyte (or Kool-Aid), cream cheese, and 3 tablespoons soda. Whip until smooth and creamy – no lumps or clumps. Now stir in the oatmeal and add another 2 tablespoons of soda. Whip thoroughly. Pour the mixture into the pie crust and even it out. Place the bowl back under a fan for another 2 hours before you cut and serve.

Everybody wants to be somebody; nobody wants to grow.
– Johann Wolfgang von Goethe

Cappuccino Crunch Cheesecake

Ingredients
1 (16 oz.) package vanilla cream cookies
1 (12 oz.) Sprite
1 1/2 coffee mugs instant milk
1/3 coffee mug French vanilla cappuccino
1/4 coffee mug sugar
1 tsp. lemon line electrolyte or 4 tbsps. Kool-Aid
3 (2 oz.) packages cream cheese
3 (1 oz.) Chick-O-Sticks

Directions
Separate the cream from the cookie and set the cream aside. Crush cookies into a fine powder and place all in a large spread bowl. Add 4 1/2 tablespoons Sprite to the bowl and knead into a pliable dough. You want the dough just moist enough to stick together. Flatten out the bottom of the bowl and, starting in the center, using your knuckles, press down firmly, working your way around the bowl, towards the outside. Dough will begin to climb the sides of the bowl. Work this into the pie crust and smooth out once done. Place the bowl under a fan to dry for 2 hours. In a separate spread bowl, combine instant milk, cappuccino, sugar, electrolyte (or Kool-Aid), cream cheese, and 5 tablespoons Sprite. Using 2 spoons, whip until smooth and creamy – no lumps or clumps. Pour this mixture into the crust and even it out. Crush Chick-O-Sticks and sprinkle evenly on top. Allow this to dry for 2 hours before you cut. Use the cream from cookies for another treat.

We are either progressing or retrograding all the while; there is no such thing as remaining stationary in this life.
– James Freeman Clarke

Banana Nut Cheesecake

Ingredients
1 pint banana nut ice cream
1 1/2 coffee mugs instant milk
2 (2 oz.) packages energy mix
1 (16 oz.) box oatmeal cream pies
2 tablespoons chocolate syrup
2 packages chocolate cupcakes

Directions
Allow the ice cream to melt. While waiting, use your ID and separate oatmeal cream pies. Use these to create a pie crust in a bowl, cream side up. Leave no gaps. Once ice cream has melted, in another spread bowl combine instant milk, chocolate syrup, and a little more than half the pint of ice cream. Whip this well. Two spoons work best, and you may need to add just a little more ice cream as you whip. You want this thick, smooth, and creamy with no lumps or clumps, like pancake batter. Remove banana chips from the energy mix and add the rest of the packages to the milk mixture and whip again. Open cupcakes and set all inside the crust. Pour the milk mixture around these. Decorate the pie with banana chips and set aside for 4 hours before you cut.

Awareness without action is worthless.
– Dr. Phil

Cupcake Cheesecake

Ingredients

1 (13 oz.) box graham crackers
1 (12 oz.) Sprite
1 coffee mug hot chocolate mix
1 1/2 coffee mugs instant milk
1 tsp. lemon lime electrolyte or 2 tbsps. Kool-Aid
3 (2 oz.) packages cream cheese
2 packages chocolate cream cupcakes

Directions

You will need 3 large spread bowls. Crush graham crackers into a fine powder and place in a large spread bowl. Add 3 tablespoons of Sprite to the bowl and knead into a pliable dough. You only want this dough moist enough to stick together. Add a drop or two more if needed. Flatten out the dough in the bottom of the spread bowl and, starting in the center, using your knuckles, press down firmly, working your way around the bowl, towards the outside. Dough will begin to climb the sides of the bowl. Work this into your pie crust and smooth out once done. Place this bowl under a fan to dry for 2 hours. In another bowl, combine hot chocolate mix with 3 1/2 tablespoons Sprite and mix well. Put this mixture in an insert cup and heat in a hot pot for the same 2 hours. Once crust is dry and hot chocolate is cooked, in a third spread bowl, combine instant milk, electrolyte, cream cheese, and 5 tablespoons Sprite. Whip thoroughly with two spoons until smooth with no lumps or clumps. Remove hot chocolate mix from hot pot, pour into crust, and even out. Open cupcakes and set them inside the pie crust. Now pour the milk mixture into the crust around the cupcakes. Place this bowl under a fan for 2 hours before you cut. This is one incredible treat.

God ever works with those who work with will.
– Aeschylus

Ice Cream Cheesecake

Ingredients
1 pint favorite ice cream
1 (16 oz.) package cream cookies (any flavor)
1 (12 oz.) Sprite
1 1/2 coffee mugs instant milk
1 teaspoon lemon lime electrolyte or 2 tablespoons Kool-Aid
1/4 coffee mug maple brown sugar instant oatmeal
3 (2 oz.) packages cream cheese
1 (2 oz.) package salted peanuts

Directions
Set the pint aside so it fully melts. Separate cream from cookies and set cream aside. Crush all cookies into a fine powder and place all in a large spread bowl. Add 4 1/2 tablespoons Sprite to the bowl and knead into a pliable dough. Flatten out the bottom of the bowl and, starting in the center, using your knuckles, press down firmly, working your way towards the outside. Dough will begin to climb the sides of the bowl. Work this into your crust and smooth out once done. Place the bowl under a fan to dry for 2 hours. Once dry, in a separate spread bowl, combine instant milk, electrolyte (or Kool-Aid), oatmeal, cream cheese, and slowly add 1/2 the ice cream as you whip. Make sure all the milk has dissolved. Once whipped, add the cream from the cookies and whip again. This will be a very thick mixture. Pour the mixture into the crust and even it out. Decorate with peanuts. Dry for 2 hours before you cut. Make sure to eat within 24 hours.

Be not afraid of growing slowly; be afraid only of standing still.
— Chinese Proverbs

Maple Syrup Cheesecake

Ingredients
1 (16 oz.) package vanilla cream cookies
1 (12 oz.) Sprite
1 1/2 coffee mugs instant milk
2 (2 oz.) packages cream cheese
1 teaspoon lemon lime electrolyte or 2 tablespoons Kool-Aid
3 tablespoons maple syrup

Directions
Separate cream from cookies and set cream aside. Crush cookies into a fine powder and place in a large spread bowl. Add 4 1/2 tablespoons of Sprite to this and knead into a pliable dough. You want the dough moist enough to stick together. Flatten the bottom of the bowl and, starting in the center, using your knuckles, press down firmly, working your way around the bowl, towards the outside. Dough will begin to climb the sides. Work this into the pie crust and smooth out once done. Place the bowl under a fan to dry for 2 hours. Once dry, using a separate spread bowl, combine instant milk, cream from cookies, cream cheese, electrolyte (or Kool-Aid) 1 tablespoon maple syrup, and 4 tablespoons Sprite. Use two spoons and whip until smooth and creamy – no lumps or clumps. Pour this mixture into the pie crust and dry for 2 hours before you cut. You can drizzle more maple syrup on the cheesecake as you serve.

> *Every day do something that will inch you closer to a better tomorrow.*
> *– Doug Firebaugh*

Troy Traylor

Dr. Pepper Cheesecake

Ingredients
1 (16 oz.) package vanilla cream cookies
1 (12 oz.) Dr. Pepper
1 teaspoon lemon lime electrolyte or 2 tablespoons Kool-Aid
1 1/2 coffee mugs instant milk
3 (2 oz.) packages cream cheese
1 (1 oz.) Chick-O-Stick

Directions
Separate the cream from the cookies and set the cream aside. Crush cookies into a fine powder and place in a large spread bowl. Add 4 1/2 tablespoons of Dr. Pepper to this and knead into a pliable dough. Flatten out the bottom of the bowl and, starting in the center, using your knuckles, press down firmly, working your way around the bowl, towards the outside. Dough will begin to climb the sides. Work this into the pie crust and smooth out once done. Place under a fan to dry for 2 hours. Once dry, in a separate spread bowl, combine electrolyte (or Kool-Aid), instant milk, cream cheese, cream from cookies, and 6 tablespoons Dr. Pepper. Whip with 2 spoons until smooth and creamy – no lumps or clumps. This will be very thick. Crush Chick-O-Stick and sprinkle on top. Allow to dry for 2 hours before you cut.

I've missed more than 9000 shots in my career. I've lost almost 300 games. 26 times I've been trusted to take the game winning shot and missed, I've failed over and over and over again in my life, and that is why I succeed.
– Michael Jordan

Strawberry Cheesecake

Ingredients
1 (16 oz.) package vanilla or Duplex cream cookies
1 (12 oz.) Sprite
1 1/2 coffee mugs instant milk
1 teaspoon lemon lime electrolyte or 2 tablespoons Kool-Aid
3 (2 oz.) packages cream cheese
1/4 (12 oz.) bottle strawberry preserves

Directions
Separate the cream from the cookies and set the cream aside. Crush cookies into a fine powder and place in a large spread bowl. Add 4 1/2 tablespoons of Sprite to this and knead into a pliable dough. You want the dough just moist enough to stick together. Flatten out into the bottom of the bowl, and starting in the center, using your knuckles, press down firmly, working your way around the bowl, towards the outside. Dough will begin to climb the sides. Smooth out once done. Place the bowl under a fan to dry for 2 hours. Once dry, in a separate spread bowl, combine cream from cookies, instant milk, electrolyte (or Kool-Aid), cream cheese, and 5 tablespoons Sprite and whip until smooth and creamy – no lumps or clumps. Pour the mixture into the pie crust and even it out. Place the bowl back under the fan for 2 hours. Just prior to cutting, spread strawberry preserves over the top. Incredible!

Our ideas, like orange-plants, spread out in proportion to the size of the box which imprisons the roots.
– Edward Bulwer Lytton

Troy Traylor

Strawberry Cheesecake #2

Ingredients
1 pint strawberry ice cream
1 (12 oz.) strawberry soda
1 (2 oz.) package cream cheese
1 (16 oz.) package Duplex cream cookies
1 1/2 coffee mugs instant milk
1 Snickers bar

Directions
Set ice cream aside to fully melt. Separate the cream from the cookies and set the cream aside. Crush cookies into a fine powder and place in a large spread bowl. Add 4 1/2 tablespoons soda to this and knead into a pliable dough, just moist enough to stick together. Flatten out the bottom of the bowl and, starting in the center, using your knuckles, press down firmly, working your way around the bowl, towards the outside. Dough will begin to climb the sides. Work this into your pie crust and smooth out once done. Place the bowl under a fan to dry for 2 hours. Place a Snickers bar in a hot pot to melt. Once the crust is dry, using a large spread bowl, combine instant milk, cream from cookies, half the ice cream, and cream cheese. Use two spoons and whip until smooth and creamy. You want this very thick, like pancake batter. To adjust, just add a little more ice cream. Set the bowl aside for 30 minutes and drizzle a Snickers bar over the top. Allow to dry for 2 hours before you cut.

It is not what a man does that determines whether his work is sacred or secular, but why he does it.
– A.W. Tozer

Fine Dining Prison Cookbook 2

Root Beer Float Pie

Ingredients
1 (13 oz.) box graham crackers
1 1/2 coffee mugs instant milk
1 (12 oz.) root beer soda
1 teaspoon lemon lime electrolyte or 2 tablespoons Kool-Aid

Directions
Crush all graham crackers into a fine powder. Add 3 tablespoons of soda to this and knead into a pliable dough, just moist enough so it sticks together. Flatten out into the bottom of the spread bowl and starting in the center, using your knuckles, press down firmly, working your way around the bowl, towards the outside. Dough will begin to climb the sides. Work this into the pie crust and smooth out once done. Place the bowl under a fan to dry for 2 hours. Once dry time is up, combine instant milk, electrolyte (or Kool-Aid), and 8 tablespoons soda in a separate spread bowl and whip until smooth and creamy – no lumps or clumps. Pour this mixture into the pie crust and even it out. Place the bowl back under a fan to dry for an additional 2 hours before cutting.

The only way to do great work is to love what you do. If you haven't found it yet, keep looking. Don't settle. As with all matters of the heart, you'll know when you find it.
– Steve Jobs

Helpful Cooking Tips

Lettuce keeps better if you store it in the refrigerator without washing it first, so that the leaves are dry. Wash the day you are going to use it.

Stuff a miniature marshmallow in the bottom of a sugar cone to prevent ice cream drips.

To keep potatoes from budding, place an apple in the bag with the potatoes.

Ground spices really should be replaced every 6 months or so! Unless you know you will use them up fairly quickly, buy a bottle in partnership with a friend and split the contents. You'll each benefit from fresh spices.

Instead of the water your recipe calls for, try juices, bouillon, or water you have cooked vegetables in. Instead of milk, try buttermilk, yogurt, or sour cream. It can add a whole new flavor and improve nutrition.

When browning ground meat, brown several pounds and drain. Divide evenly in freezer containers and freeze. Unthaw in the microwave for quick fixing next time.

Marshmallows will not dry out when frozen.

Fresh egg shells are rough and chalky; old egg shells are smooth and shiny.

Add a little lemon and lime to tuna to add zest and flavor to tuna sandwiches. Use cucumbers soaked in vinegar and pepper on a sandwich instead of tomatoes. Use mustard instead of mayo to cut the fat and add a tang.

Steak Sauce with A Kick: Deglaze your frying pan (after searing your New York steaks) with brandy. Add two tablespoons of butter, a little white wine, and a splash of Grand Marnier. Serve over steaks – you'll never use steak sauce again.

Section 17:
Candies & Treats

Troy Traylor

Armadillo Eggs

Ingredients
5 vanilla wafers
1/2 coffee mug hot chocolate mix
7 chocolate chip cookies
1 package M&Ms
3 1/2 tablespoons hot water

Directions
Crush the chocolate chip cookies and the vanilla wafers, but keep them separate. Lightly crush M&Ms. In a spread bowl, combine the chocolate chip cookies, hot chocolate mix, M&Ms, and 3 tablespoons hot water. Mix all well. The combination should be stiff and moist. You may need to add the other 3 1/2 tablespoons, but begin with 3. Divide the mixture once kneaded and roll into balls about the size of quarters. Roll balls around in vanilla wafers to coat. Place on plain white paper and set under a fan for 3 hours before you eat.

A ship is always safe at shore but that is not what it is built for.
– Albert Einstein

Baltimore's Butterscotch Brownies

Ingredients
1 (16 oz.) package double fudge cookies
2 coffee mugs hot chocolate mix
1 (7.5 oz.) package butterscotch candies
7 tablespoons hot water

Directions
Separate the cream from the cookies and set the cream aside. Crush cookies into a fine powder and place in a spread bowl. Crush all the candy into tiny pieces. Add half the candy and all but 2 tablespoons of hot chocolate mix to a bowl. Add 6 tablespoons of hot water to the bowl and knead into the pliable dough – just thick and moist, not wet. Once kneaded, place the mixture in a clean, large chip bag and flatten out evenly. Thickness is your call. Cut the bag open and allow it to dry while you make your topping. In an insert cup, combine the cream from the cookies, the rest of the candy, 2 tablespoons hot chocolate mix, and 1 tablespoon hot water. Place the insert cup in a hot pot to heat for 1 hour. Stir occasionally. Once cooked, pour icing over brownies and even out. Allow this to set for 4 hours. If you cannot obtain fudge cookies, substitute with vanilla wafers and make icing out of 2 heaping tablespoons of peanut butter, 2 tablespoons of hot chocolate mix, and 2 tablespoons of hot water.

He that will not reflect is a ruined man.
– Asian Proverb

Troy Traylor

Caramel Clusters

Ingredients
4 (2 oz.) packages salted peanuts
20 (1 oz.) Chick-O-Sticks
2 (8 oz.) Bud's Best Butterfinger cookies
6 Milky Way candy bars

Directions
Rinse salt from peanuts and pat dry. Crush all cookies and Chick-O-Sticks. Dice all candy bars into small pieces and place all in an insert cup. Place the insert in a hot pot and fully melt. Use the hottest pot available. Once candy bars are fully melted, combine all ingredients in a large spread bowl and mix well. Two spoons will work best. Once thoroughly mixed, cut open a large, clean chip bag and lay it on the bunk. Divide the mixture into pieces, approximately 50, and lightly press down on each. No certain shape. Allow these to set up and dry for 3-4 hours before you eat. What an awesome treat!

The mind is everything. What you think is what you become.
– Buddha, Spiritual Leader

Chocolate Covered Marshmallow Treats

Ingredients
2 plain Hershey candy bars
4 vanilla moon pies (large)
1 heaping teaspoon peanut butter
1 (2 oz.) package salted peanuts

Directions
Dice the candy bar into small pieces and place all in an insert cup, along with the peanut butter. Place the insert cup into a hot pot to heat until all is melted, approximately 45 minutes. Separate the marshmallow part from the cookie part. Cut the marshmallows into 4 pieces each. Rinse salt from peanuts and pat dry. Lightly crush these peanuts. After the mixture is melted, place the marshmallow pieces in a spread bowl, pour the insert mixture over the top, and top with peanuts. Allow this to set up and dry for 3 hours before you eat. You can eat the cookie parts of the moon pies separately.

Everyone is gifted, but some people never open their package.
– Wolfgang Riebe

Troy Traylor

Chocolate Munchkins

Ingredients
1 (16 oz.) package Duplex cream cookies
1 tablespoon cheap coffee
2 heaping tablespoons peanut butter
5 tablespoons hot water

Directions
Separate the cream from the cookies and set the cream aside. Crush cookies into a fine powder and place in a large spread bowl. Add peanut butter to the bowl. Combine coffee and hot water in your coffee mug and mix. Spoon 4 tablespoons of coffee into a bowl and knead this into the pliable dough, thick and moist. Divide the mixture into equal parts of about 20. Roll all into balls. Place on plain white paper while you make the topping. In your insert cup, combine the cream from the cookies and 1 tablespoon of hot coffee, and place in a hot pot to melt for 1 hour. Stir occasionally. Once the cream is ready, drizzle it over the munchkins and dry for another 2 hours. These are delicious!

What do you do with a mistake: recognize it, admit it, learn from it, forget it.
– Dean Smith

Chocolate Popcorn Balls

Ingredients
1/2 coffee mug hot chocolate mix
2 (2 oz.) packages salted peanuts
5 tablespoons hot water
1 (6 oz.) bag buttered popcorn

Directions
In a large spread bowl, combine hot chocolate mix and hot water. Use two spoons to mix thoroughly. This will be a very thick mixture. Now add peanuts to the popcorn bag and pour in the hot chocolate mixture. Knead until all is mixed and coated. Divide the mixture into 4 equal parts and roll into balls. Place back in the spread bowl and place the bowl under a fan to dry for 2 hours. These make a nice little treat.

It is better to be healthy alone than sick with someone else.
– Dr. Phil

Cream Filled Chocolate

Ingredients
3 (16 oz.) packages vanilla wafers
1/4 coffee mug hot water
1 (3.5 oz.) package vanilla whey
4 coffee mugs hot chocolate mix
2 (2 oz.) packages cream cheese
2 heaping tablespoons peanut butter

Directions
Crush all vanilla wafers as fine as possible. Split this between 2 large spread bowls. Equally divide the hot chocolate mix between bowls as well. Add 6 tablespoons of hot water to each bowl and knead well. These ingredients have to be thoroughly mixed. You want a moist and stiff mixture. Once both bowls are kneaded, get 2 large clean chip bags and place one bowl of mixture in each bag. Flatten out bags and even them out. Cut both bags open and allow them to dry while preparing the filling. In an insert cup, combine cream cheese, vanilla whey, peanut butter, and 5 tablespoons hot water. Whip well and place in a hot pot to heat for 1 hour. Once cooked, evenly spread the mixture over one of the wafer mixtures. Place the other wafer mixture on top. If you're a baller and want to add a box of oatmeal cream pies, split all pies in half with an ID card and cover the top, cream side down. Allow this to dry for 2 hours before cutting and serving. Enjoy!

Progress is impossible without change, and those who cannot change their minds cannot change anything.
– George Bernard Shaw

Crunchy Chewy Granola

Ingredients
5 tablespoons hot chocolate mix
1 (2 oz.) package trail mix
1/2 coffee mug maple brown sugar instant oatmeal
2 tablespoons peanut butter
4 tablespoons cold water
1/2 coffee mug regular instant oatmeal

Directions
In a large spread bowl, combine just 2 tablespoons of hot chocolate mix with all the remaining ingredients and knead very well. Once kneaded, divide the mixture into 10 equal-sized parts and roll up into balls. Place the rest of the hot chocolate mixture in a small spread bowl and roll the balls in the mix to coat each one. Allow to set up and dry for 2-3 hours before you eat. Grab some coffee – you'll love these.

*A sensible person accepts correction,
but you can't beat sense into a fool.
– Proverbs 17:10 CEV*

Troy Traylor

Coffee Delights

Ingredients
1 (16 oz.) package cream cookies (any flavor)
1 package nutty bars
1 oatmeal cream pie
1 coffee mug hot coffee
5 tablespoons hot chocolate mix
3 tablespoons peanut butter

Directions
Separate the cream from the cookies and set the cream aside. Crush cookies as fine as possible. Crush a nutty bar and mash an oatmeal cream  pie. Combine these three ingredients in a large spread bowl, add 4 1/2 tablespoons hot coffee to the bowl, and knead into a pliable dough. You may need to add another 1/2 tablespoon of coffee, but you do not want this too wet – only moist enough to stick together. Divide the mixture into equal parts and roll into a ball. Make these about the size of half dollars. Use your thumb and press an indentation in each ball. Place all on plain white paper. Now combine the cream from the cookies, hot chocolate mix, peanut butter, and 2 1/2 tablespoons of hot coffee in a small bowl or cup. Whip until smooth, creamy, and very thick, like icing. Fill in indentations with about a half tablespoon each. Place all under a fan to dry for 4 hours before you eat.

*The more you praise and celebrate your life,
the more there is in life to celebrate.
– Oprah*

Dirty Mudslide

Ingredients
1 (16 oz.) package Duplex cream cookies
2 vanilla moon pies (large)
1 package nutty bars
1/2 Butterfinger candy bar
2 tablespoons hot water
3 Milky Way candy bars
2 tablespoons peanut butter

Directions
Separate the cream from the cookies and set the cream aside. Divide cookies by color. You will not use the vanilla parts. Crush the chocolate parts as fine as possible. Place this in a large spread bowl with 1 1/2 tablespoons hot water and knead into a dough-type substance. Now, separate this into three equal parts and roll into balls. These should be small enough to fit inside an insert cup. Take moon pies and separate the marshmallow from the cookie part. You will not use cookie parts. Crush the nutty bars in the package. Cut candy bars into small pieces. Layer in this order in your insert cup: 1 cookie ball, 1 marshmallow, half the candy bar pieces, half the nutty bars, 1 tablespoon peanut butter. Now top with another cookie ball and repeat steps once again. Top with the last cookie ball, and crush Butterfinger to decorate. Place the insert in a hot pot for 3 hours. Use the hottest pot available. These are incredible! Save cookie cream for another treat.

Winning isn't everything, it is the only thing.
– Vince Lombardi

Troy Traylor

Min-choca Drops

Ingredients
1 (16 oz.) package Duplex cream cookies
3 (1 oz.) mint sticks
6 tablespoons hot water
1/2 teaspoon coffee

Directions
Separate the cream from the cookies and set the cream aside. Crush all cookies into a fine powder and place in a spread bowl. Crush mint sticks into tiny pieces. Add the mint sticks, 5 tablespoons of water, and coffee to the bowl and knead into the pliable dough, just moist enough so that it all sticks together. Once kneaded, divide the mixture into equal parts, not too big, not too small. Roll each piece into a ball. Place all on plain white paper to dry while making the topping. In an insert cup, combine the cream from the cookies and 1 tablespoon of hot water. Whip and place in a hot pot to heat for an hour. Once the cream is ready, whip well and drizzle over the cookie mixture. Allow to set up and dry for another 2 hours before you eat.

If you would not be forgotten, as soon as you are dead and rotten, either write things worth reading, or do things worth writing.
– Benjamin Franklin

One Sweet Treat

Ingredients
2 (16 oz.) packages vanilla cream cookies
1 (12 oz.) Coca-Cola
4 coffee mugs hot chocolate mix
1/2 (18 oz.) jar peanut butter
3 tablespoons butter
50 (1 oz.) Chick-O-Sticks
1 1/2 tablespoons hot water

Directions
You will need 1 thick, small trash bag and 2 large, spread bowls. Separate the cream from the cookies and set the cream aside. Crush cookies as fine as possible. Using two separate spread bowls, equally combine half the cookies, a 1/4 of the Coca-Cola, half the hot chocolate mix, and half the peanut butter. Knead each bowl thoroughly. Do not be afraid to get your hands dirty. Once kneaded, cut open the trash bag and lay it on your bunk. Use butter to coat the bag. Empty one bowl at a time onto the bag and use a jar or soda can to roll out the mixture. You want the mixture on the thin side. Open all Chick-O-Sticks and one by one, wrap the hot chocolate mixture around each one. Now, place the cream from the cookies in an insert cup with 1 1/2 tablespoons hot water. Heat insert cup in a hot pot for 1 hour, stirring occasionally. Once cooked, whip well and drizzle over each treat. Allow this to set up and dry for 3 hours before you eat. You'll make lots of friends with these!

I can't change the many years of yesterday, but I can do something about my tomorrow.
– Jackie Kucera

Troy Traylor

Oooie-Gooey & Chewy

Ingredients
1 (8 oz.) bag Bud's Best Butterfinger cookies
3 Milky Way candy bars
10 (1 oz.) Chick-O-Sticks

Directions
Crush all cookies and Chick-O-Sticks and put in a large spread bowl. Now cut up all candy bars into small pieces and put it into an insert cup. Place the insert cup in a hot pot to heat until all is fully melted. Once all is melted, pour into spread bowl and mix well using two spoons. Cut open a clean, large chip bag and place it on the bunk. Divide the cookie mixture into 20-25 pieces and roll into balls. You can flatten them a little with a spoon or the palm of your hand. Allow these to set up and dry for 3 hours before you eat.

Show me a gracious loser, and I'll show you a failure.
– Knute Rockne

Fine Dining Prison Cookbook 2

Strawberry Dream Treats

Ingredients
1 (16 oz.) package strawberry cream cookies
1/2 coffee mug strawberry and cream instant oatmeal
1 (12 oz.) strawberry soda
2 (2 oz.) packages cream cheese
1 light teaspoon strawberry Kool-Aid

Directions
Separate cream from cookies and set cream aside. Crush cookies as fine as possible and put in a large spread bowl. Add oatmeal and 5 tablespoons of soda to the bowl and knead into a pliable dough. You only want the dough moist enough to stick together. Place this mixture in a clean chip bag and flatten out evenly. Cut the bag open and let it dry while making the topping. In a small bowl or cup, combine the cream from the cookies, the cream cheese, and 1 tablespoon soda. Whip until smooth and creamy. Spread this mixture over the cookie mixture and sprinkle Kool-Aid over the top as decoration. These have an unbelievable taste.

Our task must be to free ourselves from this prison by widening our circles of compassion to embrace all living creatures and the whole of nature in its beauty.
– Albert Einstein

Troy Traylor

Sweet Treat 2

Ingredients
1/2 (13 oz.) box graham crackers
1 heaping tablespoon peanut butter
1/4 coffee mug hot water
12 (1 oz.) mint sticks or fruit sticks
1 coffee mug hot chocolate mix
1 (10 pack) box instant oatmeal
(about 2 1/2 coffee mugs)
3 tablespoons butter

Directions
You will need 1 thick, small trash bag. Crush the graham crackers as fine as possible and set aside. In a large spread bowl, combine hot chocolate mix, peanut butter, oatmeal, and hot water. It is best to begin with a little water at a time until you have a really thick mixture. Mix well with a spoon, then knead with your hands until thoroughly mixed. Once kneaded, cut open the trash bag, lay one of them on your bunk, and coat it with butter. Pour the mixture from the bowl onto the trash bag and use a jar or soda can to roll out the mixture fairly thin. Now open all the mint (or fruit) sticks and one by one roll the hot chocolate mixture around each one. Now you can place the crushed graham crackers in a spread bowl or a clean chip bag and, one by one, roll each treat in graham crackers to coat. Allow treats to set up and dry for 3 hours before you eat.

*We cannot go back and make a new start,
but we can start now and make a new ending.
– Franklin Covey*

Section 18:
Bars of All Kinds

Baltimore's Best Bars

Ingredients
2 (16 oz.) packages cream cookies (any flavor)
10 (1 oz.) Chick-O-Sticks
2 packages M&Ms
1 (10 packs) box instant oatmeal (about 2 1/2 coffee mugs)
3 serving raisins from tray (about 3/4 coffee mug)
1/2 (18 oz.) jar peanut butter
3/4 coffee mug hot water

Directions
Separate cream from cookies and set cream aside. Crush all cookies as fine as possible and crush Chick-O-Sticks. Set M&Ms aside for a moment and combine all other ingredients in a large spread bowl. Knead well. Now use cookie trays and fill the form bars. Place plain white paper on the bed or desk. Turn cookie trays upside down and start at one end to push out bars onto paper. Allow bars to sit for 6-8 hours. About 1 hour before the bars are dry, place the cream from the cookies in an insert cup with 1 1/2 tablespoons of water. Heat the insert cup in a hot pot for an hour. Stir occasionally. Once bars are dry, whip icing and pour evenly over the top of the bars. Now decorate bars with M&Ms. Allow these to sit for another 2 hours before you eat.

Shoot for the moon and if you miss you will still be among the stars.
– Les Brown

Big House Bars

Ingredients
1 (16 oz.) bag vanilla wafers
1/2 (18 oz.) jar peanut butter
4 (2 oz.) packages salted peanuts
1 (10 pack) box instant oatmeal (about 1 1/2 coffee mugs)
1 (10 oz.) bag sunflower seeds (about 1 1/2 coffee mugs)
3 packages plain M&Ms
1/4 coffee mug hot water

Directions
Crush vanilla wafers as fine as possible. In a clean, large chip bag, combine all the ingredients and knead well. Grab a couple of cookie trays and fill them with the mixture to form bars. Place clean white paper on the bunk or bed. Turn cookie trays upside down and press on one end to work bars out onto the paper. Allow these to sit for at least 6-8 hours, but it's best to let them sit overnight. These are a great treat.

Troubles impending always seem worse than troubles surmounted, but that does not prove that they really are.
– Arthur M. Schlesinger

Troy Traylor

Candy Bars

Ingredients
3 (16 oz.) packages cream cookies (any flavor)
1 (16 oz.) bag vanilla wafers
6 (2 oz.) packages salted peanuts
30 (1 oz.) Chick-O-Sticks
1 (2 lbs.) bag hot chocolate mix (about 4 coffee mugs)
1 (10 oz.) bag sunflower seeds (about 1 1/2 coffee mugs)
1/2 (18 oz.) jar peanut butter
2 (12 oz.) cherry Dr. Peppers

Directions
You will need a large trash bag or 3 large spread bowls. Separate cream from cookies and set cream aside. Crush all cookies and wafers as fine as possible. Crush Chick-O-Sticks. If you're using a trash bag, combine all ingredients and knead thoroughly. If using bowls, equally divide the ingredients between bowls and knead well. Once all is kneaded, grab a few cookie trays and fill with the mixture to form bars. Place some plain white paper on the desk or the bunk. Turn trays upside down and start at one end and work bars out onto paper. Dry these for 6-8 hours, but overnight is best. Once bars are dried, place the cream from the cookies in an insert cup with 1 1/2 tablespoons hot water. Heat the insert cup in a hot pot for 1 hour. Stir occasionally. Now pour this icing over bars and dry for another 2 hours. This is an awesome treat that you will love.

To choose one's attitude in a given set of circumstances is to choose one's own way.
– Victor Frankl

Cereal Bars

Ingredients
1 (20 oz.) bag Frosted Mini Wheats cereal
1 coffee mug hot chocolate mix
1 (10 pack) box instant oatmeal (about 2 1/2 coffee mugs)
1/4 coffee mug sunflower seeds
1/2 (18 oz.) jar peanut butter
5 (2 oz.) packages peanuts or trail mix
1/4 coffee mug hot water

Directions
You can use two separate spread bowls for this or a large cheese puff bag. Crush cereal well and combine all the ingredients together, and knead thoroughly. If you use two bowls, equally divide all between the bowls. Make sure this is kneaded well. You do not want the mixture off balance. Use cookie trays and fill them to make bars. Put some clean white paper on your bunk and turn the trays upside down. Start on the end to push the bar out. Place all on paper and set under a fan for 6-8 hours to dry. They are better if you allow them to sit overnight. You will be surprised at how delicious these are.

Always do your best. What you plant now, you will harvest later.
– Og Mandino

Troy Traylor

Mint Chocolate Bars

Ingredients
10 (1 oz.) mint sticks
1/2 coffee mug hot water
3 (3 oz.) Ramen noodles (any flavor)
1 (12 oz.) cherry Dr. Pepper
1 (2 lbs.) bag hot chocolate mix (about 4 coffee mugs)

Directions
Crush all mint sticks and place in an insert cup with 2 tablespoons hot water. Stir well and place in a hot pot for 1 1/2 hours to fully melt. Stir occasionally. While all is melting, use a bottle or other implement to fully crush Ramen into a powder. This takes a little work and is best accomplished by crushing 1/3 at a time in the soup bag. Place the powder in a large spread bowl with 1/2 a coffee mug of hot water to hydrate. Cover the powdered Ramen with the melted mint sticks. It is best to have a large trash bag, but you can use 3 separate spread bowls. Just evenly divide the chocolate mix and Dr. Pepper between bowls. Combine all ingredients and knead well. Now, grab a couple of cookie trays and form bars. Place plain white paper on the desk or the bunk, turn the trays upside down, and push the bars out onto the paper. Dry these for 6-8 hours, but overnight is best. Scrumptious!

*The gem cannot be polished without friction,
nor man perfected without trial.
– Confucius*

Section 19:
Fudge

Troy Traylor

Baltimore's Fabulous Fudge

Ingredients
4 (3 oz.) Ramen noodles (any flavor)
2 (16 oz.) packages vanilla or Duplex cream cookies
15 (1 oz.) Chick-O-Sticks
1 (12 oz.) Coca-Cola
6 oatmeal cream pies
1 1/2 coffee mugs instant oatmeal (any flavor)
4 coffee mugs hot chocolate mix
4 (2 oz.) packages salted peanuts
1 1/2 tablespoons cheap coffee
up to 1 coffee mug hot water

Directions
You will need a large, thick trash bag or 3 large spread bowls. Crush Ramen noodles into a super fine powder. It is best to use a full cheese bottle and crush 1/3 at a time in its bag. It takes work and time. Separate the cream from the cookies and set the cream aside. Now, crush all cookies into a fine powder. Crush all Chick-O-Sticks as well. In a large trash bag, combine all the ingredients except the cream from cookies, coffee, and 1/4 coffee mug of the hot water. Knead this thoroughly. If using spread bowls, just equally divide the mixture and knead separately. The mixture will be very thick and stiff. Shape mixture into about a 10" x 6" block. Cut open the bag and allow it to dry overnight. Flavors really set in. In the morning, combine the cream from cookies, coffee, and 2 tablespoons hot water in an insert cup. Place the insert in a hot pot to heat for 1 hour. Stir occasionally. Once ready, pour this over the fudge and spread evenly. Allow this to cool for 1 1/2 hours. Cut to size with your ID. Just as the recipe states, this is fabulous.

The greatest thing in the world is not so much where we stand as in what direction we're moving
– Oliver Wendell Holmes

Fine Dining Prison Cookbook 2

Butterfinger Delight Fudge

Ingredients
30 vanilla wafers
4 tablespoons hot chocolate mix
1 (3.5 oz.) package vanilla whey
3 macaroon cookies
1 Butterfinger candy bar
1/4 coffee mug regular oatmeal
3 tablespoons instant milk
4 heaping tablespoons chocolate syrup
5 tablespoons hot water

Directions
Crush vanilla wafers and place in a large spread bowl. Add oatmeal, hot chocolate mix, and 1 tablespoon hot water to the bowl and mix well. In a separate spread bowl, combine instant milk, vanilla whey, chocolate syrup, and 4 tablespoons hot water. Mix well. Crush macaroon cookies and add to the milk mixture. Mix well. Combine both bowls and knead together. This is your dough. Place the mixture in a large chip bag and flatten out like a pizza. Cut open the bag and crush the Butterfinger on top. Allow to air dry 4-6 hours. Use ID and cut into squares.

No act of kindness, no matter how small, is ever wasted.
– Aesop

Helpful Cooking Tips

Sunlight doesn't ripen tomatoes; warmth does. Store tomatoes with stems pointed down, and they will stay fresher, longer.

Place green fruits in a perforated plastic bag. The holes will allow air to circulate while retaining the ethylene gas that fruits produce during ripening.

For fluffier, whiter rice, add one teaspoon of lemon juice per quart of water. To add extra flavor and nutrition to rice, cook it in the liquid reserved from cooking vegetables.

Save all kinds of leftover bread, bagels, baguettes, sandwich loaves, rolls, crackers, biscuits, and buzz to very fine crumbs in the food processor. Freeze in self-sealing plastic bags and use for stuffing and toppings.

To peel thin-skinned fruits and vegetables easily, place them in a bowl and cover with boiling water, let stand for one minute, then peel with a sharp paring knife.

For an easy dressing for fruit salad, try a grated orange rind and orange juice added to sour cream.

Cream won't curdle when poured over fruits if you add a pinch of baking soda with the cream before serving.

If you add a small pat of butter when cooking fruit for jams and jellies, you won't have any foam to skim off the top.

If you have a problem with fruit jellies not setting, place the jars in a shallow pan half filled with cold water, then bake in a moderate oven for 30 minutes.

For attractive individual butter servings, squeeze butter through a pastry bag or plastic bag onto a cookie sheet, set in the refrigerator to harden.

Section 20:
Cookies

Candy Oatmeal Cookies

Ingredients
2 heaping tablespoons peanut butter
3/4 coffee mug regular oatmeal
5 tablespoons hot water
1 Three Musketeers candy bar
3/4 coffee mug maple brown sugar oatmeal

Directions
Using your insert cup, combine peanut butter and a candy bar. You can cut it up if you desire. Heat these ingredients in the insert cup in a hot pot until fully melted. While waiting, in a large spread bowl combine remaining ingredients and mix well. Once the mixture in the hot pot is melted, pour it into a spread bowl and use a spoon to mix well. Divide the mixture into 12 pieces and roll into balls. Line the desk or bunk with plain white paper and place all balls on the paper. Use your palm and flatten out into cookies. Allow these to sit for 2-3 hours before you eat. These are great with a hot cup of coffee.

Fall seven times, stand up eight.
– Japanese Proverb

Chocolate Drop Sugar Cookies

Ingredients
2 (16 oz.) packages vanilla wafers
9 tablespoons hot water
1 coffee mug hot chocolate mix
5 teaspoons sweetener or 8 tablespoons sugar
1/2 (3 oz.) Ramen noodles (any flavor)
1 (12 oz.) Coca-Cola

Directions
Crush vanilla wafers as fine as possible and put them in a large spread bowl. Add sweetener and hot water, and knead into a thick, pliable dough. Use a full cheese bottle and crush Ramen into a fine powder, 1/4 at a time, in its bag. Using a separate spread bowl, combine Ramen, hot chocolate mix, and a 1/4 coffee mug of soda and mix very well. Set this bowl aside for a moment. Now divide the cookie mixture into several pieces and roll into balls. Place plain white paper on the desk or the bunk. Place balls on paper and, using your thumb, press a dent into each ball. Carefully take the hot chocolate mix and fill in these dents. It is okay if it runs down the sides of balls. You can use your spoon and flatten these a little or leave as munchkins. Allow drying for 2-3 hours before you eat. Your creativity will be well appreciated by all.

What I must do is all that concerns me.
– Ralph Waldo Emerson

Chocolate Oatmeal Cookies

Ingredients
6 tablespoons butter
4 teaspoons sweetener or 8 tablespoons sugar
1/2 coffee mug instant milk
1/3 coffee mug hot chocolate mix
1 (10 pack) box instant oatmeal (about 2 1/2 coffee mugs)
1/2 coffee mug of peanut butter

Directions
In a clean rice bag, combine butter, sweetener, instant milk, and hot chocolate mix. Place in a hot pot to fully heat. Add no water; butter will be your liquid. Stir occasionally. It takes about 1 hour. Once everything is melted, combine all the ingredients in a large spread bowl and use two spoons to mix well. Divide the mixture into 12 pieces and roll up into balls. Line a desk or a bunk with plain white paper, and place balls on the paper. Use your palm to flatten out into cookies. Allow these to dry for 2-3 hours. They are so good!

When life gives you lemons, make lemonade
– Elbert Hubbard

Fine Dining Prison Cookbook 2

Fudge Cookies

Ingredients
3 (16 oz.) packages cream cookies (any flavor)
1 (16 oz.) box oatmeal cream pies
1 (2 lb.) bag hot chocolate mix (about 4 coffee mugs)
1 (12 oz.) Coca-Cola

Directions
You will need 1 thick, small trash bag or 3 large spread bowls. Separate the cream from all cookies and set the cream aside. Crush all cookies as fine as possible. If using a trash bag, combine all ingredients and knead thoroughly. If using spread bowls, equally divide ingredients and knead well. You want this mixture to be moist and stick together. If it is too dry, add a few spoons of water. Once kneaded, divide the mixture and roll into balls about the size of a ping-pong ball. Line a desk or a bunk with plain white paper and place balls onto the paper. Now use your palm and flatten out into cookies.

Allow to dry for about 3-4 hours. One hour prior to dry time, place all the cream from the cookies in an insert cup with 2 tablespoons of water. Place the insert cup into a hot pot. Heat the insert for 1 hour, stirring occasionally. Drizzle this mixture over cookies and let stand for 1 more hour. Heat up the coffee and invite an associate or two – you'll have plenty.

Nothing contributes so much to tranquilize the mind as a steady purpose – a point on which the soul may fix its intellectual eye.
– Mary Shelley

Troy Traylor

Peanut Butter Cookies

Ingredients
1 (13 oz.) box graham crackers
1/2 (18 oz.) jar peanut butter
4 tablespoons hot water
2 (2 oz.) packages salted peanuts
3/4 coffee mug maple brown sugar oatmeal

Directions
Crush all graham crackers and place in a large spread bowl. Combine remaining ingredients in the bowl, mix well, and knead thoroughly. Divide the mixture into 12 equal pieces. Roll into balls. Line desk or bunk with plain white paper. Place balls on paper and use a spoon or palm to flatten out into cookies. Allow these to dry for 3-4 hours. Heat up the coffee and eat up. This is a great way to begin or end a day.

Constant dripping hollows out a stone.
– Lucretius

Section 21:
Puddings

Troy Traylor

Chocolate Pudding

Ingredients
4 large chocolate moon pies
4 tablespoons butter
8 tablespoons hot water
2 Milky Way candy bars
1 (16 oz.) bag vanilla wafers
1 (2 oz.) package salted peanuts (optional)

Directions
Separate the marshmallow parts from the cookie. Crush the cookie parts and dice the marshmallow parts. In an insert cup, combine cookie parts, marshmallow pieces, and butter. Heat the insert cup in a hot pot until fully melted. Use the hottest pot available. Crush vanilla wafers while you wait. Once the insert cup is ready, using a large spread bowl, combine the wafers and the insert cup mixture with the hot water. Thoroughly mix. If you use the optional peanuts, put them on top now and lightly mix again. Cover and allow to sit for 1 hour.

For hope is but the dream of those that wake.
– Matthew Prior

Banana Pudding

Ingredients
1 box banana moon pies (mini) or 6 large moon pies
4 heaping tablespoons butter
1 (16 oz.) bag vanilla wafers
8 tablespoons hot water
2 (2 oz.) packages energy mix (optional)

Directions
Separate the marshmallow from the cookie part. Dice the marshmallow and crush the cookie parts. In an insert cup, combine the marshmallow pieces and butter. Place the insert cup into a hot pot for 1 1/2 hours to fully melt. Stir occasionally. Crush vanilla wafers while you wait. Place vanilla wafers in a large spread bowl. Once the insert cup is ready, pour the mixture into the crushed wafers and add the hot water. Stir this well. Now add the energy mix if using and stir well again. Eat while warm or allow to cool for a bit.

Nothing great was ever achieved with enthusiasm.
– Ralph Waldo Emerson

Troy Traylor

Lemon Pudding

Ingredients
1 (16 oz.) bag vanilla wafers
2 teaspoons sweetener or 4 tablespoons sugar
1 (12 oz.) Sprite (will use just 3/4 can)
3/4 coffee mug instant milk
1 tsp. lemon lime electrolyte or 2 tbsps. lemon Kool-Aid

Directions
Crush half the bag of vanilla wafers and set the other half aside. In a large spread bowl, combine the remaining ingredients and whip the mixture well. Layer a separate spread bowl with half the remaining wafers and top with half the milk mixture. Repeat once
again. Place the bowl under a fan to set up for 1 1/2 hours. Dig in!

We are still masters of our fate.
We are still captains of our souls.
– Winston Churchill

Another Chocolate Pudding

Ingredients
1 (16 oz.) package double fudge or chocolate cream cookies
1 coffee mug hot chocolate mix
2 teaspoons sweetener or 4 tablespoons sugar
3/4 coffee mug instant milk
1 (12 oz.) Coca-Cola (will only use 1/2 can)

Directions
Separate cream from cookies and set cookies aside. In a large spread bowl, combine hot chocolate mix, sweetener, cookie cream, instant milk, and Coca-Cola. Whip this mixture until smooth and creamy. Once smooth, pour the mixture into a rice bag and heat the bag in a hot pot for 1 hour. Stir occasionally. You may need to add a tad more soda as it heats. Once ready, layer a spread bowl with cookies and pour a little hot chocolate mixture over the top. Repeat until all the ingredients are used. Allow to sit for 2 hours prior to eating.

I will love the light because it shows me the way, yet I will endure the darkness because it shows me the stars.
– Og Mandino

Conversion Chart

Liquid Measurements

Gallons	Quarts	Pints	Cups	Fluid Ounces
1 gal.	4 qt.	8 pt.	16 cups	128 fl. oz.
1/2 gal.	2 qt.	4 pt.	8 cups	64 fl. oz.
1/4 gal.	1 qt.	2 pt.	4 cups	32 fl. oz.
1/8 gal.	1/2 qt.	1 pt.	2 cups	16 fl. oz.
1/16 gal.	1/4 qt.	1/2 pt.	1 cup	8 fl. oz.

Dry Measurements

Cups	Tablespoons	Teaspoons	Ounces	Grams
1 cup	16 tbsp.	48 tsp.	8 oz.	229 g.
3/4 cup	12 tbsp.	36 tsp.	6 oz.	171 g.
2/3 cup	10 2/3 tbsp.	32 tsp.	5.34 oz.	152 g.
1/2 cup	8 tbsp.	24 tsp.	4 oz.	114 g.
1/3 cup	5 1/2 tbsp.	16 tsp.	2.67 oz.	76 g.
1/4 cup	4 tbsp.	12 tsp.	2 oz.	57 g.
1/8 cup	2 tbsp.	6 tsp.	1 oz.	29 g.
1/16 cup	1 tbsp.	3 tsp.	.5 oz.	14 g.

1 Coffee Mug = 12 oz.

Shopping List

Candies

Butterscotch	7.5 oz. bag
Candy bars	regular size
Chick-O-Sticks	1 oz.
Fireballs	6 oz. bag (about 32 pieces)
Fruit/Mint Sticks	1 oz.
M&Ms	1.74 oz.
Orange slices	10.25 oz. bag
Pastries	Large individual package
Penny Candy	8 oz. bag (assorted flavors)
Pie (cherry/lemon)	4 oz. (4" x 2" box)

Chips/Crackers

BBQ Chips	8 oz. bag
Cheese Nips	18 oz. box
Cheese Puffs	11 oz. bag
Cheetos	2 oz. bag
Corn Chips	16 oz. bag
Golden Round Crackers	13.7 oz. box (4 sleeves)
Hot Fries	1.25 oz. bag
Jalapeno Chips	8 oz. bag
Nacho Chips	3 oz. bag
Matzo Crackers	16 oz. package
Packaged Crackers	1.375 oz. package
Party Nix	11 oz. bag
Pork Skins	2.75 oz. bag
Regular Potato Chips	2 oz./8 oz. bag
Salsa Verde Chips	6 oz. bag
Saltine Crackers	4-sleeve box
Shabang Chips	8 oz. bag
Tortilla Chips	16 oz. bag

Condiments

BBQ Sauce	18 oz. bottle
Butter	16 oz. squeeze bottle
Chili Con Queso	15 oz. bottle

Chili Garlic Sauce	8 oz. bottle
Cream Cheese	4 tbsps. = 2 oz. package
Garlic Powder	1.75 oz. bottle
Habanera/hot Sauce	8 oz. bottle
Honey	8 oz. bottle
Jalapeno Pepper	1.3 oz. single package
Jelly-Grape	12 oz. bottle
Ketchup	20 oz. bottle
Mustard	14 oz. bottle
Onion Flakes	1.75 oz. bottle
Onion Powder	1.75 oz. bottle
Peanut Butter	18 oz. jar
Pepper	shaker
Picante Sauce	12 oz. bottle
Pickle (large dill)	single package, about 9 oz.
Pickle Juice	from single package
Ranch Dressing	4 tbsps. = 2 oz. package
Relish	8 oz. jar
Salad Dressing	15 oz. jar
Salsa	8 oz. bottle
Salt	shaker
Sandwich Spread	15 oz. bottle
Seasoning Packet	from Ramen noodles
Soy Sauce	5 oz. bottle or homemade
Spice-Coriander & Annatto	1.5 oz. bag
Squeeze Cheese	16 oz. bottle
Strawberry Preserves	12 oz. bottle
Sugar (brown/white)	misc. tsp/tbsps.
Sweetener	100 count box

Cookies

Bud's Best (variety flavors)	8 oz. bag
Cookies (various)	12 oz. package
Cookies (filled)	16 oz. package
Graham Crackers	13 oz. box
Maria Cookies	5.6 oz. package

Regal Graham	8 oz. package
Vanilla Wafers	16 oz. package

Drinks

Creamers (variety flavors)	12 oz. bag
Electrolyte Drink Mix	1 tsp = 0.14 pack
Hot Chocolate Mix	10 oz. bag
Instant Cappuccino	12 oz. bag
Instant Coffee (all)	4 oz. bag
Instant Milk	4 oz. bag
Instant Tea Bags	100 count box
Juices/Soda	12 oz. cans
Kool-Aid	19 oz. jug
Water (cold/hot)	misc. coffee mugs
Whey/Chike	tsp/tbsp/misc.

Little Debbie's/Misc. Sweets

Chocolate Covered Peanuts	8 oz. bag
Cup Cakes	2 per package
Donut Sticks	10 oz. box
Malt balls	3 oz. bag
Moon Pies	2.75 oz. singles
Nutty Bars	12 oz. box
Oatmeal Cream Pies	16 oz. box
Rice Crispy Treats	4.75 oz. box
Swiss Rolls	12 oz. box

Miscellaneous

Beef & Cheese Stick	single serving pkg
Cereal (misc. flavors)	20 oz. bag
Corn Bread	misc. amount
Chocolate Syrup	16 oz. bottle
Corn Nuts	6 oz. bag
Energy/Trail Mix	2 oz. bag
Flour Tortillas	10 oz. pack
Hard Boiled Eggs	misc. amount
Hot/Salted/Unsalted Peanuts	2 oz. bag
Ice Cream	individual bar/pint

Instant Brown Rice	6.5 oz. bag
Instant Oatmeal	10 pack box
Instant Potatoes	4 oz. bag
Instant White Rice	8 oz. bag
Pancakes	misc. amounts
Pasta Kit	size not available
Ramen Noodles	3 oz. bag
Red Beans & Rice	4.6 oz. package
Refried Beans	15 oz. bag
Scrambled Eggs	misc. amounts
Sliced Bread	loaf
Sunflower Seeds	10 oz. bag
Tray Serving-Fruit	4 oz.
Tray Serving-Meat	8 oz.
Tray Serving-Vegetables	4 oz.

Packaged Meat

Beef Stew	11.25 oz. package
Beef Tips in Gravy	8 oz. package
Chicken Chili	11.25 oz. package
Chicken Chunks	7 oz. package
Chili with/without Beans	11.25 oz. package
Mackerel (Regular/Siracha)	3.5 oz. package
Mexican Beef	8 oz. package
Pepperoni Slices	3.5 oz. package
Pink Salmon	5.6 oz. package
Pot Roast	11.25 oz. package
Sardine (Regular/Siracha)	3.53 oz. package
Shredded Beef in BBQ Sauce	11.25 oz. package
Spam	3 oz. package
Summer Sausage	5 oz. package
Tomato Basil Soup Mix	15 oz. package
Tuna in Jalapenos	3.53 oz. package
Tuna – Regular	4.23 oz. package
Turkey Bites	4 oz. package

This shopping list does not include ingredients needed for the bonus section. Due to the fact that some states may not sell the same size packages, I have done my best to give you a breakdown by coffee mugs (12 oz.), teaspoons, and tablespoons. A little more or less won't affect the recipe. Adjust to your own liking.

This has been a remarkable journey, and I have enjoyed every step of the way. I pray that you truly enjoy these creations and discover a few of your own along the way.

There is a total of 130 ingredients in these recipes.

Helpful Cooking Tips

To keep your pizza crust crispy, try placing the cheese on before the sauce.

To save leftover wines, freeze them in ice cube trays. They can be used for any dish you would season with wine, or can also be used in coolers.

Cottage cheese can be used in place of sour cream when making dips. Just place it in the blender until it is creamy.

Cream cheese can be colored with liquid food coloring as a filler for dainty rolled sandwiches. Try a different color for each layer and slice as you would a jelly roll.

Freeze red and green maraschino cherries in ice cubes. You can also do this with cocktail onions, mint leaves, or green olives for martinis.

French fries will be deliciously golden brown if sprinkled with flour before frying.

To bake the perfect potato, rub butter over the potatoes before baking to prevent the skin from cracking and to improve the taste.

For the best gourmet French fries, let cut potatoes stand in cold water for an hour before frying. Dry well before cooking. The trick is to fry them twice. The first time, just fry them for a few minutes and drain off the grease. The second time, fry them until golden brown.

To tell how old an egg is, place the egg in a pan of cold water. If it lies on its side, it is fresh – if it tilts on an angle, it's approximately 3-4 days old – if an egg stands upright, it is probably about 10 days old. If an egg floats to the top, it is old and should not be used.

Hard-boiled eggs will slice better if you wet the knife in water before cutting.

Bonus Section:
A Few Secrets from the Outside

(For Foodies, Thrifty Cooks, and Curious People Everywhere)

Troy Traylor

Avocado Deviled Eggs with Prosciutto Leaves

Ingredients
1 dozen hard-boiled eggs
2 avocados, peeled and diced
2 tablespoons mayonnaise
1 teaspoon sea salt
2 tablespoons finely diced onion
1 chive, cut into thin strips
2 tablespoons finely diced red, yellow, and orange peppers
3 ounces thinly sliced prosciutto

Directions
Cut eggs in half lengthwise and scoop yolks into the bowl of a stand mixer. Add diced avocados, mayonnaise, and sea salt. Whip until ingredients are completely incorporated, about 3 minutes. Place the avocado mixture into a pastry bag and pipe into the hollow of the eggs. Top with diced onion, chives, and pepper mixture. Cover and chill. Heat oven to 400°F. Cut prosciutto into leaf shapes and place on a rimmed baking sheet. Place in oven for 3 minutes or until "leaves" begin to crisp. Allow to cool. Decorate each deviled egg with a leaf (or two) of crispy prosciutto. Makes 24 deviled eggs.

> *Live as if you were to die tomorrow.*
> *Learn as if you were to live forever.*
> *– Mahatma Gandhi*

Baked Pancetta Baskets with Tomatoes, Crab, and Egg

Ingredients
8 thin slices pancetta
8 ounces lump crabmeat
1 teaspoon salt
4 tablespoons Quick Hollandaise (recipe follows)
2 Roma tomatoes, sliced
4 jumbo eggs
1 teaspoon pepper

Directions
Heat oven to 350°F. In a muffin tin, place 2 slices pancetta in each of 4 wells, overlapping on the bottom to form a basket. Place 2 slices of tomato on top of the pancetta in each basket. Add 2 ounces of crab to each basket and crack one jumbo egg on top of each. Season with salt and pepper. Place the pan in the preheated oven for 5 to 7 minutes until the egg is at the desired doneness. Serve immediately or refrigerate. Plating: Place 2 tablespoons of Quick Hollandaise and set the pancetta basket on top. Garnish with fresh herbs, as desired. Quick Hollandaise: In a blender, combine 4 egg yolks, 1 tablespoon lemon juice, 1 1/4 teaspoons Dijon mustard, and 1/8 teaspoon hot sauce. Blend on high for 15 seconds until completely combined. In a glass measuring cup, heat 1/2 cup butter for 2 minutes in the microwave until very hot. Setting the blender on high, pour very hot butter into the egg mixture in a thin stream. Use immediately. Makes 4 servings.

That which does not kill us makes us stronger.
– Friedrich Nietzsche

Troy Traylor

Barbecue Chicken with Corn Bread Topper

Ingredients
1 1/2 lbs. cooked boneless skinless chicken breast and thighs
1 can (about 15 ounces) red beans, rinsed and drained
1 cup chopped green bell pepper
1 can (8 ounces) tomato sauce
1/2 cup barbecue sauce
1 package (6 ounces) corn bread mix (plus ingredients)

Directions
Preheat oven to 375°F. Spray a microwavable 8-inch baking dish with nonstick cooking spray. Dice chicken. Combine chicken, beans, bell pepper, tomato sauce, and barbecue sauce in a prepared dish. Loosely cover with plastic wrap or waxed paper. Microwave on medium-high (70%) 8 minutes or until heated through, stirring halfway through. Meanwhile, prepare corn bread mix according to package directions. Spoon batter over the chicken mixture. Bake 15 to 18 minutes or until a toothpick inserted into the center of the corn bread layer comes out clean. Makes 8 servings.

Be who you are and say what you feel, because those who mind don't matter and those who matter don't mind.
– Bernard M. Baruch

Barley and Swiss Chard Skillet Casserole

Ingredients
1 cup water
1 cup chopped green bell pepper
3/4 cup uncooked quick-cooking barley
1/8 teaspoon garlic powder
1/8 teaspoon red pepper flakes
2 cups packed coarsely chopped Swiss chard
1 cup canned reduced-sodium navy beans, rinsed, and drained
1 cup quartered cherry tomatoes
1/4 cup chopped fresh basil
1 tablespoon olive oil
2 tablespoons Italian-seasoned dry bread crumbs

Directions
Preheat broiler. Bring water to a boil in a large skillet; add bell peppers, barley, garlic powder, and red pepper flakes. Reduce heat; cover and simmer 10 minutes or until liquid is absorbed. Remove from heat. Stir in chard, beans, tomatoes, basil, and oil. Sprinkle with breadcrumbs. Broil 2 minutes or until golden. Fresh spinach or beet greens can be substituted for Swiss chard. Makes 8 servings.

> *We must not allow other people's limited perceptions to define us.*
> *– Virginia Satir*

Bone Broth-Braised Beef Short Ribs with Rosemary and Thyme

Ingredients
4 pounds beef short ribs
2 tablespoons olive oil
1 teaspoon pepper
3 sprigs fresh thyme
2 cups beef bone broth
2 tablespoons butter
1 teaspoon salt
3 sprigs fresh rosemary
2 cups dry red wine

Directions
Heat oven to 275°F. Put a Dutch oven on medium heat on the stovetop. Add short ribs, butter, and olive oil. Sear all sides of the short ribs. Remove short ribs and set aside. Add salt, pepper, rosemary, thyme, and red wine to the pot and bring the mixture to a boil. Allow to boil for 2 minutes. Add bone broth and bring the mixture back to a boil. Add reserved ribs and place covered Dutch oven into preheated oven for 3 1/2 hours. Makes 4 servings.

Do what you can, with what you have, where you are.
– Theodore Roosevelt

Candy Cane Cookie Bars

Ingredients
1 cup (2 sticks) butter, room temperature
1 1/2 cups sugar
2 eggs
1 1/2 teaspoons vanilla
3 1/2 cups flour
1/2 teaspoon baking soda
1/2 teaspoon salt
45 finely-chopped candy cane Hershey's Kisses (1.5 cups)
cream cheese frosting (recipe follows)
additional, chopped candy cane Kisses for garnish (optional)

Directions
Heat oven to 350°F. Line a 9 x 13-inch baking dish with parchment paper or spray it with cooking spray. In a large mixing bowl, beat the butter and sugar until light and fluffy. Add eggs and vanilla and mix until combined. In a separate bowl, whisk the flour, baking soda, and salt. Slowly add the flour mixture to the egg mixture and mix. Gently fold in the chopped Hershey's Kisses. Press dough into the baking dish. Bake for 18 to 20 minutes or until edges begin to have a touch of golden brown. Remove from the oven and let the bars cool in the pan. When completely cool, frost with Cream Cheese Frosting and sprinkle with chopped kisses to garnish. Makes 24 bars.

Cream Cheese frosting: With an electric mixer, beat 4 ounces of room-temperature cream cheese and 1/2 cup of room-temperature butter until light and fluffy. Add 2 1/2 cups powdered sugar and 1/2 teaspoon vanilla extract and beat until creamy. (The mixture may seem dry at first, but it will become creamy after being beaten for a while.) Add 2 to 3 tablespoons of milk, 1 tablespoon at a time, until the frosting reaches the desired consistency.

Cheddar Bacon Scallion Drop Biscuits

Ingredients
2 cups flour
1/2 teaspoon baking soda
2 tablespoons baking powder
7 tablespoons whole milk
1 egg
1/2 cup chopped, cooked bacon
1/2 teaspoon kosher salt
8 tablespoons melted butter (divided use)
1/4 cup sour cream
1/4 cup diced scallions
1 cup shredded mild cheddar cheese
pinch of sugar

Directions
Heat oven to 400°F. Combine the flour, sugar, baking soda, salt, and baking powder in a large bowl. Stir well. Add 7 tablespoons of melted butter, milk, and sour cream into the flour mixture. Stir well. In a small bowl, crack the egg and lightly whisk. Add the egg to the biscuit batter. Stir well to combine. Add the scallions, bacon, and the cheddar to the dough. Stir well to combine. Using an ice cream scoop (or 2 spoons), spoon out dollops of dough into a parchment- or Silpat-lined baking sheet. Place biscuits about 1/2 inch apart. Use the remaining tablespoon of melted butter to brush on top of the biscuits. Place the biscuits into the oven and cook 13 to 15 minutes (or until golden and cooked all the way through). Remove from the oven and place on a cooling rack. Serve warm. Makes 18 to 20 biscuits.

Be yourself; everyone else is already taken.
– Oscar Wilde

Fine Dining Prison Cookbook 2

Crab Canapes Appetizer

Ingredients
2/3 cup fat-free cream cheese, softened
2 teaspoons lemon juice
1 teaspoon hot pepper sauce
1 package (8 ounces) imitation crabmeat, flaked
1/3 cup chopped red bell pepper
2 green onions with tops, sliced (about 1/4 cup)
64 cucumber slices (about 2 1/2 medium cucumbers)
chopped fresh parsley (optional)

Directions
Combine cream cheese, lemon juice, and hot pepper sauce in a medium bowl, and mix well. Stir in Crabmeat, bell peppers, and green onions. Cover and refrigerate for at least 1 hour to allow flavors to blend. When ready to serve, spoon 1 1/2 teaspoons crabmeat mixture onto each cucumber slice. Garnish with parsley. Makes 16 servings.

This above all: to thine own self be true.
– William Shakespeare

Troy Traylor

Egg Cobb Tower with Grilled Chicken Breast

Ingredients
1 bunch kale, ribs removed, rough chopped
2 avocados, diced
2 Roma tomatoes, diced
2 hard-boiled eggs, diced
1/2 pound bacon, cooked and diced
5 ounces blue cheese crumbles
2 tbsps. finely chopped fresh herbs (such as parsley and chives)
4 to 5 ounces grilled chicken breast, chilled
8 tablespoons Citrus Yogurt Dressing (recipe follows)

Directions
In a large bowl, fold together Kale, avocados, tomatoes, eggs, bacon, and blue cheese. Add fresh herbs and toss. Divide the mixture among 4 plating rings (available on Amazon for $19.99 for a set of four) and chill for at least 30 minutes to assist in maintaining shape when served. Slice chicken. Plating: Place 2 tablespoons of Citrus Yogurt Dressing, top with a ring of Kale Cobb and fan-grilled chicken. Garnish with tomato, if desired.

Citrus Yogurt Dressing: Zest and juice 2 lemons and 1 orange. In a medium bowl, whisk the juice and zest with 1 cup plain Greek yogurt, 1/3 cup apple cider vinegar, 3 tablespoons olive oil, and 1 tablespoon parsley. Add 1 teaspoon salt and 1/2 teaspoon pepper, adjusting to taste. Store under refrigeration.

If you cannot do great things, do small things in a great way.
– Napoleon Hill

Frosted Cold-Brew Shortbread

Ingredients
2/3 cup butter, room temperature
1/2 teaspoon vanilla extract
1 1/4 cups flour
1/2 cup powdered sugar
1 tablespoon instant coffee granules
Cold-Brew Frosting (recipe follows)
2 ounces chocolate candy coating for drizzle (see note)

Directions
Heat oven to 325°F. In a mixing bowl, cream together the butter and vanilla extract with an electric mixer. Slowly mix in flour, powdered sugar, and coffee granules. Place the dough between 2 sheets of parchment paper dusted with flour. With a rolling pin, roll dough to 1/2-inch thickness. Remove the paper and use a cookie cutter to cut into round circles. Place on baking sheets. Bake for 15 minutes. Cool completely and frost with Cold-Brew Frosting. Melt chocolate candy coating in a double boiler or in a microwave, using short bursts of power and stirring in between. Drizzle. Makes 2 dozen cookies.

Cold-Brew Frosting: Whisk together 1 cup powdered sugar with 2 tablespoons Cold-Brew coffee.

Note: Chocolate candy coating (almond bark) can be found in the baking aisle or baking supply stores.

If opportunity doesn't knock, build a door.
– Milton Berle

Goat Cheese & Tomato Omelet

Ingredients
3 egg whites
2 eggs
1 tablespoon water
1/8 tablespoon salt
1/8 tablespoon black pepper
nonstick cooking spray
1/3 cup crumbled goat cheese
1 medium plum tomato, diced
2 tablespoons chopped fresh basil or parsley

Directions
Whisk together egg whites, eggs, water, salt, and pepper in a medium bowl. Spray a medium nonstick skillet with cooking spray; place over medium heat. Add egg mixture; cook 2 minutes or until eggs begin to set on bottom. Lift edges of omelet to allow uncooked portion of egg to flow underneath. Cook 3 minutes or until the center is almost set. Sprinkle cheese, tomato, and basil in the center of the omelet. Fold half of the omelet over the filling. Cook for 1 to 2 minutes, or until the cheese begins to melt and the center is set. Cut the omelet in half and transfer to a serving plate. Makes 2 servings.

Wise men speak because they have something to say; fools because they have to say something.
– Plato

Greek Chicken & Spinach

Ingredients
Nonstick cooking spray
1 cup finely chopped onion
1 package (10 ounces) chopped spinach, squeezed dry
1 cup uncooked-quick-cooking brown rice
1 cup water
1/4 teaspoon salt
1/8 teaspoon ground red pepper
3/4 pound chicken tenders
2 tsps. dried Greek seasoning (oregano, rosemary, and sage)
1/2 teaspoon salt-free lemon-pepper seasoning
1 tablespoon olive oil
1 lemon, cut into wedges, to serve

Directions
Preheat oven to 350°F. Lightly coat a large ovenproof skillet with cooking spray, heat over medium heat. Add onion; cook and stir 2 minutes or until translucent. Add spinach, rice, water, salt, and red pepper. Stir until well blended. Remove from heat. Place chicken on top of the mixture in a skillet in a single layer. Sprinkle with Greek seasoning and lemon-pepper seasoning. Cover with foil. Bake 25 minutes or until the chicken is no longer pink in the center. Remove foil. Drizzle oil evenly over the top. Serve with lemon wedges. Makes 4 servings.

Whenever you find yourself on the side of the majority, it is time to pause and reflect.
– Mark Twain

Troy Traylor

Hot Chicken Sheet Pan Fajitas

Ingredients
3/4 cup Cholula hot sauce, or your favorite hot sauce
juices from 1 lime
1 tablespoon chili powder
1/2 bunch cilantro, rough chopped
5 tablespoons canola oil (divided use)
2 onions, halved and sliced
tortillas for serving
3 tablespoons orange juice
1 teaspoon ground cumin
4 garlic cloves, crushed
2 tsps. kosher salt (divided use)
2 pounds chicken breast, cut into thin slices
3 bell peppers, seeded and sliced

Directions
Add hot sauce, cilantro, 1 teaspoon salt, and 3 tablespoons canola oil to a large bowl or baking pan. Mix well. Add the chicken and stir to coat. Cover and refrigerate for 1 hour, up to 8 hours. Remove the chicken from the fridge 30 minutes before cook time. Place an oven rack in the highest slot in the oven. Heat the broiler to 550°F. Line a baking sheet with foil. Add the onions and bell peppers. Top them evenly with the remaining 2 tablespoons of canola oil and the remaining 1 teaspoon of salt. Toss to incorporate. Spread the mixture into one even layer. Place in the

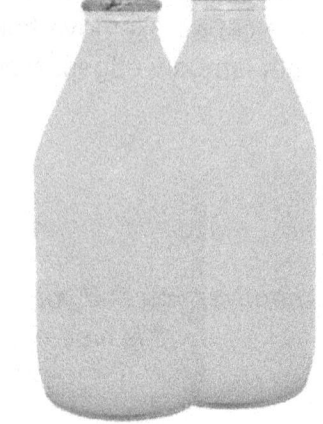

oven and broil for 10 minutes or until the vegetables are browned and blistered. Remove and toss the vegetables. With a slotted spoon, add the chicken tenders to the sheet pan, layering evenly on top of the vegetables. Place into the oven and broil for 5 to 8 minutes, or until the chicken reaches an internal temperature of 165°F. Remove from the oven and serve with tortillas. Makes 8 servings.

No pressure... No diamonds.
*– **Thomas Carlyle***

Troy Traylor

Jalapeno and Caramelized Onion Mashed Potatoes

Ingredients
1 1/2 cups half-and-half
8 tablespoons unsalted butter
2 garlic cloves, crushed
7 jalapenos, seeded and diced, plus stems
2 tablespoons extra-virgin olive oil
2 onions, halved and thinly sliced
2 1/2 tablespoons kosher salt (divided use)
10 cups peeled and diced Yukon Gold Potatoes
1/4 cup sour cream

Directions
In a small saucepan, warm the half-and-half, butter, garlic, and jalapeno stems over low heat. Heat thoroughly for 15 to 20 minutes. Set aside. Place the olive oil into a medium skillet. Add 1 layer of onions and season evenly with 1/2 teaspoon kosher salt. Cook on medium-low heat for 45 minutes. Stir occasionally. Add the jalapenos and stir well. Cook for an additional 15 minutes. Set aside. Meanwhile, bring a large pot of water to a boil and add the potatoes. Cook until tender. Strain the water. Place the potatoes back onto the stove. With a potato masher, mash the potatoes. Add 1 1/2 teaspoons kosher salt and stir well. Strain the half-and-half and butter mixture into the mashed potatoes, and discard solids. Stir well and continue to mash out any chunks of boiled potatoes. Add the jalapeno-onion mixture and sour cream to the mashed potatoes. Stir well until all the ingredients are well incorporated. Salt to taste and serve warm. Makes 10 servings.

Life shrinks or expands in proportion to one's courage.
– Anais Nin

Lemon-Raspberry French Toast

Ingredients
1 loaf (16 ounces) French bread, cut into 22, 1-inch slices
3 eggs
grated peel and juice of 2 lemons
1/4 cup packed brown sugar
3 cups fresh raspberries
2 egg whites
3 cups fat-free (skim) milk
1/4 teaspoon ground nutmeg

Directions
Spray a 13 x 9-inch baking dish with nonstick cooking spray. Arrange bread in a single layer in a baking dish. Whisk eggs, egg whites, lemon peel, and lemon juice in a medium bowl until well blended. Whisk in milk, brown sugar, and nutmeg until smooth and well blended. Pour evenly over bread slices. Refrigerate, covered, overnight. Preheat oven to 375°F. Meanwhile, let the dish stand at room temperature. Bake 35 to 40 minutes or until top begins to brown. Top evenly with raspberries. Bake 10 to 12 minutes or until a knife inserted into the center comes out clean. Let stand 5 minutes before cutting and serving. Makes 12 servings.

A journey of a thousand leagues begins beneath one's feet.
— Lao Tzu

Lentil Chili

Ingredients
1 tablespoon canola oil
4 cloves garlic, minced
1 tablespoon chili powder
1 can (32 ounces) reduced-sodium vegetable broth
3/4 cup dried brown or green lentils, rinsed and sorted
2 teaspoons smoked Chipotle hot pepper sauce
2 cups peeled and dried butternut squash
1 can (about 14 ounces) no-salt-added diced tomatoes
1/2 cup chopped fresh cilantro
1/4 cup pepitas (pumpkin seeds) (optional)

Directions
Heat oil in a large saucepan over medium heat. Add garlic; cook and stir 1 minute. Stir in chili powder; cook and stir 30 seconds. Add broth, lentils, and hot pepper sauce; bring to a boil over high heat. Reduce heat to low; simmer 15 minutes. Stir in squash and tomatoes; continue simmering 18 to 20 minutes or until lentils and squash are tender. Ladle into bowls; top with cilantro and pepitas, if desired.

Take Note! Lentils are not only a good source of iron and protein but are packed with dietary fiber. The soluble fiber in lentils helps to stabilize blood sugar levels, while the insoluble fiber is known to lower cholesterol levels and promote digestive health. Pepitas add a nice crunch to the meal for an additional 36 calories, 3 grams of fat, 2 grams of protein, and less than 1 gram of carbohydrate (for 2 1/2 tsps.). They're a good source of plant steroids, which have been found to promote heart health. Makes 5 servings.

> *What you do speaks so loudly that I cannot hear what you say.*
> *– Ralph Waldo Emerson*

Fine Dining Prison Cookbook 2

Mango Smoothie

Ingredients
2 cups frozen mango chunks, plus additional for garnish
2 containers (6 ounces each) low-fat vanilla yogurt
3/4 cup orange juice
1 teaspoon vanilla (optional)
juice of 1/2 lime
pinch salt

Directions
Combine all ingredients in a blender and blend until smooth. Pour into 4 glasses. Garnish with additional mango chunks.

Take Note! Mangoes are an excellent source of vitamin A and are a very good source of vitamin C. They also provide potassium and fiber, and they are sodium-free. If you can't find frozen mango cubes, you can make your own. Cut mango into 1-inch chunks, place on a cookie sheet, and freeze for 3 hours. Makes 4 servings.

You must be the change you wish to see in the world.
– Mahatma Gandhi

Troy Traylor

Olive Twists Appetizer

Ingredients
1 package (11 oz.) refrigerated breadstick dough (12 breadsticks)
1 egg white, beaten
12 pimiento-stuffed green olives, chopped
paprika

Directions
Preheat oven to 375°F. Line a baking sheet with parchment paper. Separate breadstick dough into individual sticks. Brush dough lightly with egg white; sprinkle with olives and paprika. Twist each stick 3 or 4 times, and place on a prepared baking sheet. Bake 11-13 minutes or until golden. Makes 12 servings.

Believe and act as if it were impossible to fail.
– Charles Kettering

Pumpkin Spice Smoothie

Ingredients
1 frozen banana
2 to 3 ice cubes
1/4 cup canned pumpkin
1/4 cup vanilla Greek yogurt
1 cup low-fat or nonfat milk (or almond milk)
1 scoop vanilla whey protein powder

Directions
Combine all ingredients in a blender and blend until smooth.

*The difference between ordinary and extraordinary
is that little extra.
– Jimmy Johnson*

Roasted Brussels Sprouts with Peppers

Ingredients
1 pound Brussels sprouts, halved
1/4 red pepper, cut into strips
1/4 yellow pepper, cut into strips
1/4 orange pepper, cut into strips
2 ounces prosciutto, chopped
2 tablespoons olive oil
2 tablespoons butter, melted
shaved Parmesan cheese, for serving

Directions
Heat oven to 450°F. On a rimmed baking sheet, spread Brussels sprouts, peppers, and prosciutto. Drizzle olive oil and butter over the vegetables. Place in oven for 5 minutes, or until desired doneness. Serve garnished with shaved Parmesan, if desired. Makes 4 servings.

The best way to predict the future is to invent it.
– Alan Kay

Roasted Vegetables with Tahini Dressing

Ingredients
8 carrots peeled and halved lengthwise
1 head cabbage cut into 8 to 10 wedges
12 radishes, thickly sliced
1 red onion, cut into bite-size wedges
1/4 cup extra-virgin olive oil
2 teaspoons kosher salt
juice of 1 lemon
1/2 cup Tahini Dressing (recipe follows)
pita bread, for serving
1/4 cup Greek yogurt

Directions
Heat oven to 425°F. Line a baking sheet with foil. Place vegetables on the sheet in one layer (this helps with even roasting). Drizzle with olive oil and salt. Place in the oven and roast for 35 to 40 minutes. While vegetables roast, make the Tahini Dressing. Remove the vegetables from the oven and drizzle with fresh lemon juice. Turn off the oven. Put the desired number of pitas into the oven and let them warm for 2 to 3 minutes. Remove the pitas, fill with vegetables, and drizzle with Tahini Dressing and Greek yogurt.

Tahini Dressing: Combine 1/3 cup plain yogurt, 1/4 cup tahini, 1/4 teaspoon ground coriander, 1/2 teaspoon kosher salt, 3 tablespoons fresh lemon juice, 2 finely chopped garlic cloves and 2 tablespoons extra virgin olive oil in a bowl. Whisk until well combined. Store in an airtight container in the fridge for a week. Yep, one week. Makes 6 servings.

Believe you can and you're halfway there.
– Theodore Roosevelt

Seasoned Pan-Seared Pork Tenderloin

Ingredients
2 pork tenderloins (about 4 pounds total)
2 tablespoons Montreal steak seasoning
2 tablespoons butter
2 tablespoons olive oil
simple pan sauce (recipe follows)
fresh herbs, for garnish

Directions
Heat oven to 325°F. Season the tenderloins with steak seasoning. In a cast iron pan, over medium heat, add butter and olive oil, and then sear tenderloins on all sides. Place skillet in the oven and bake for 15 minutes until internal temperature reaches 145° F. Remove pan from oven and allow meat to rest for 5 minutes. Slice and serve with simple pan sauce and fresh herbs, if desired. Makes 8 servings.

Simple pan sauce: Heat the pan used to cook the pork over medium heat and deglaze with 4 tablespoons butter. Continue stirring and scraping while adding 2 tablespoons brandy. Bring the mixture to a boil. Remove from heat and finish sauce with 2 tablespoons heavy cream and fresh herbs to taste.

How wonderful it is that nobody needs wait a single moment before starting to improve the world.
– Anne Frank

Fine Dining Prison Cookbook 2

Smoked Salmon Appetizers

Ingredients
1/4 cup reduced-fat or fat-free cream cheese, softened
1 tablespoon chopped fresh dill or 1 teaspoon dried dill weed
1/8 teaspoon ground red pepper
4 ounces thinly sliced smoked salmon
24 melba toast rounds or other low-fat crackers
fresh dill sprigs and chopped red onion (optional)

Directions
Combine cream cheese, dill, and red pepper in a small bowl; stir to blend. Spread evenly over each slice of salmon. Roll up salmon slices, jelly-roll style. Place on a plate; cover with plastic wrap. Chill at least 1 hour or up to 4 hours before serving. Cut salmon rolls crosswise into 3/4-inch pieces with a sharp knife. Place rolls cut side down on melba toast. Garnish each salmon roll with a dill sprig and an onion, if desired. Serve cold or at room temperature. Makes 2 dozen appetizers.

*Imagination is everything.
It is the preview of life's coming attractions.
– Albert Einstein*

Turkey and Pumpkin Skillet Lasagna

Ingredients
1 large can (29 ounces) pure pumpkin puree
1 egg
3/4 cup ricotta
1/3 cup sliced fresh sage
10 no-boil lasagna noodles
6 herbed turkey meatballs, chopped
1 cup shredded mozzarella

Directions
In a large bowl, mix pumpkin, egg, ricotta, and sage. Spread 1 cup in a large ovenproof skillet. Layer the noodles, meatballs, and pumpkin mixture. Repeat twice. Add 1 cup of water, cover, and simmer over medium heat for 10 minutes. Add cheese. Bake at 425°F, uncovered, until noodles are cooked, about 15 minutes.

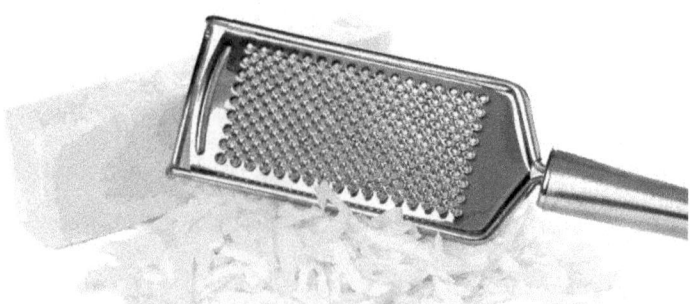

*Happiness is not something ready-made.
It comes from your own actions.*
– Dalai Lama

White Chocolate Pecan Ginger Bars

Ingredients
8 tablespoons unsalted butter
8 ounces finely crushed gingersnaps, about 2 cups
1 teaspoon ground ginger
1/2 cup flaked coconut
1/2 cup finely chopped crystallized ginger
1 cup white chocolate chips
1 cup cinnamon chips (recipe follows)
1 (14.5 ounce) can sweetened condensed milk
1 cup finely chopped pecans

Directions
Heat oven to 325°F. Lightly grease a 13 x 9-inch baking dish. Beat butter in bowl with electric mixer for about 2 minutes. Add crushed gingersnaps and ground ginger. Press the mixture into the bottom of the greased baking dish. Spread flaked coconut and chopped crystallized ginger over gingersnap crust. Sprinkle white chocolate chips and cinnamon chips over the coconut layer. Pour the sweetened condensed milk over the chips. Sprinkle the chopped pecans evenly over the condensed milk layer. Bake for 25 to 30 minutes until a toothpick inserted in the center comes out with soft crumbs (do not overbake). Cool in the pan and cut into small squares. Makes 3 dozen.

Note: Use a food processor to crush the gingersnaps or put them in a large plastic bag and use a rolling pin. Cinnamon chips are available in the baking aisle of major grocery stores. Alternatively, substitute 1 cup white chocolate chips

mixed with 1 teaspoon ground cinnamon or make your own (recipe follows).

Cinnamon chips: Heat oven to 225°F. Combine 1/2 cup white sugar, 2 teaspoons ground cinnamon, 1 tablespoon shortening, and 1 tablespoon light corn syrup. Roll mixture between 2 layers of parchment to 1/8 to 1/4-inch thickness. Transfer to a baking sheet, remove the parchment layer, and bake until golden and bubbly, about 35 minutes. Cool completely and break into pieces.

> *Remember that happiness is a way of travel,*
> *not a destination.*
> *– Roy M. Goodman*

Fine Dining Prison Cookbook
150 Secrets from "The Inside"

There are many people on the inside, as well as those of you on the outside, that love to cook a delicious tasty meal, with ordinary low-cost ingredients. This cookbook is designed to meet the needs and desires to do just that.

Many of the recipes have been developed by prisoners, for prisoners, however these recipes can also be enjoyed by college students, foodies, and thrifty cooks. These recipes have been compiled and shared from all over the U.S.A. Everyone, everywhere, can enjoy fine dining, no matter what their budget. No matter who you are or where you come from there is something for everyone, that will leave you craving for more.

Making good food is a pleasure but sharing it with those around you makes it even better. The Fine Dining Prison Cookbook has all you need to prepare easy recipes, new taste sensations and a little encouragement along the way.

Fine Dining Prison Cookbook is filled with hundreds of great recipes. The recipes are divided into ten sections.

- ★ Tasty Drinks
- ★ Condiments, Dips & Creamy Spreads
- ★ Side Dishes & Quick Snacks
- ★ Gumbos & Chowders
- ★ Meals for Every Craving
- ★ A Few Delicious Pizzas
- ★ Mexican Delights
- ★ Cakes & Pies of All Kinds
- ★ A Few Cheesecakes
- ★ Sweets & Treats of All Kinds

Only $15.99
plus $7 S/H with tracking
SOFTCOVER, 6"x 9", 232 pages

What makes Fine Dining Prison Cookbook better than others?

Bonus Content included inside Fine Dining Prison Cookbook: inspiring quotes, tidbits of knowledge, food history, monthly foodie holidays and national food days.

No Order Form Needed: Clearly write on paper & send with payment of **$22.99** to:

Freebird Publishers
221 Pearl St., Ste. 541 , North Dighton, MA 02764
Diane@FreebirdPublishers.com www.FreebirdPublishers.com

Fine Dining Prison Cookbook 2

CURRENT FULL COLOR CATALOG

98 Pages filled with books, gifts and services for prisoners

We have created four different versions of our new catalog A: Complete B:No Pen Pal Content C:No Sexy Photo Content D:No Pen Pal and Sexy Content. Available in full Color or B&W (please specify) please make sure you order the correct catalog based on your prison mail room regulations. We are not responsible for rejected or lost in the mail catalogs. Send SASE for info on stamp options.

Freebird Publishers Book Selection Includes:

- Ask. Believe. Receive.: Our Power to Create Our Own Destiny
- Celebrity Female Star Power
- Cell Chef 1 & 2
- Cellpreneur: The Millionaire Prisoner's Guidebook
- Chapter 7 Bankruptcy: Seven Steps to Financial Freedom
- Convicted Creations Cookbook
- Cooking With Hot Water
- DIY for Prisoners
- Federal Rules of Criminal Procedures Pocket Guide
- Federal Rules of Evidence Pocket Guide
- Fine Dining Cookbook 1, 2, 3
- Freebird Publisher's Gift Look Book
- Get Money: Self Educate, Get Rich, & Enjoy Life (3 book series)
- Habeas Corpus Manual
- Hobo Pete and the Ghost Train
- Hot Girl Safari: Non-Nude Photo Book
- How to Write a Good Letter From Prison
- Ineffective Assistance of Counsel
- Inmate Shopper
- Inmate Shopper Censored
- Introduction to Financial Success
- Kitty Kat: Adult Entertainment Resource Book
- Life With a Record
- Locked Down Cookin'
- Locked Up Love Letters: Becoming the Perfect Pen Pal
- Parent to Parent: Raising Children from Prison
- Penacon Presents: The Prisoners Guide to Being a Perfect Pen Pal
- Pen Pal Success: The Ultimate Guide to Getting & Keeping Pen Pals
- Pen Pals: A Personal Guide for Prisoners
- Pillow Talk: Adult Non-Nude Photo Book
- Post-Conviction Relief Series (Books 1-7)
- Prison Health Handbook
- Prison Legal Guide
- Prison Picasso
- Prisoner's Communication Guidelines for Navigating in Prison
- Prisonyland Adult Coloring Book
- Pro Se Guide to Legal Research & Writing
- Pro Se Prisoner: How to Buy Stocks and Bitcoin
- Pro Se Section 1983 Manual
- Section 2254 Pro Se Guide to Winning Federal Relief
- Soft Shots: Adult Non-Nude Photo Book
- The Best 500 Non-Profit Organizations for Prisoners & Their Families
- Weight Loss Unlocked
- Write & Get Paid

CATALOG ONLY $5 - SHIPS BY FIRST CLASS MAIL
ADDITIONAL OPTION: add $5 for Shipping and Handling with Tracking

PayPal — VISA DISCOVER BANK

NO ORDER FORM NEEDED CLEARLY WRITE ON PAPER & SEND PAYMENT TO:
FREEBIRD PUBLISHERS 221 Pearl St., Ste. 541, North Dighton, MA 02764
www.FreebirdPublishers.com Diane@FreebirdPublishers.com Text/Phone: 774-406-8682
We accept all forms of payment. Plus Venmo & CashApp! Venmo: @FreebirdPublishers   CashApp: $FreebirdPublishers

2 MUST HAVE BOOKS FOR PRISONERS

$29.99
$20.99 plus $9 Shipping/Handling with Tracking

$26.99
$17.99 plus $9 Shipping/Handling with Tracking

NO ORDER FORM NEEDED
Clearly write on paper and send with payment.
Freebird Publishers, 221 North Dighton, MA 02764

INMATE SHOPPER

EVERY ISSUE CONTAINS:
- Non-Nude Girls
- Pen Pal Resources
- Social Media
- Magazine Sellers
- Text/Phone
- Catalogs to Order
- Sexy Photo Sellers
- Typists
- Personal Assistants
- Gift Shops
- Publishing Services
- LGBTQ Resources

GET BOTH FOR JUST **$47.99** INCLUDES PRIORITY S/H WITH TRACKING

THE BEST 500+

INCLUDES MANY RESOURCES:
- Legal: Innocence, Research, Advocates, Copies
- Newsletters
- Educational
- Health & Healthcare
- Reentry & Jobs
- Family & Children
- Veterans
- Sentencing Issues
- LGBTQ Resources
- Newsletter & Books
- & Much Much More!

ALSO AVAILABLE FOR PURCHASE AT FREEBIRDPUBLISHERS.COM

FREEBIRDPUBLISHERS.COM

Rate Us & Win!

We do monthly drawings for a FREE copy of one of our publications. Just have your loved one rate any Freebird Publishers book on Amazon and then send us a quick e-mail with your name, inmate number, and institution address and you could win a FREE book.

FREEBIRD PUBLISHERS
221 Pearl St., Ste. 541
North Dighton, MA 02764

www.freebirdpublishers.com
Diane@FreebirdPublishers.com

Troy Traylor

FREEBIRD PUBLISHERS

Thanks for your interest in Freebird Publishers!

We value our customers and would love to hear from you! Reviews are an important part in bringing you quality publications. We love hearing from our readers-rather it's good or bad (though we strive for the best)!

If you could take the time to review/rate any publication you've purchased with Freebird Publishers we would appreciate it!

If your loved one uses Amazon, have them post your review on the books you've read. This will help us tremendously, in providing future publications that are even more useful to our readers and growing our business.

Amazon works off of a 5 star rating system. When having your loved one rate us be sure to give them your chosen star number as well as a written review. Though written reviews aren't required, we truly appreciate hearing from you.

Sample Review Received on Inmate Shopper

 poeticsunshine

★★★★★ **Truly a guide**
Reviewed in the United States on June 29, 2023
Verified Purchase

This book is a powerhouse of information. My son had to calm/ground himself to prioritize where to start.

www.ingramcontent.com/pod-product-compliance
Lightning Source LLC
Chambersburg PA
CBHW070735170426
43200CB00007B/530